S0-AHD-514

Children and Number

Children and Number

*Difficulties in Learning
Mathematics*

MARTIN HUGHES

Basil Blackwell

© Martin Hughes 1986

First published 1986

Basil Blackwell Ltd
108 Cowley Road, Oxford OX4 1JF, UK

Basil Blackwell Inc.
432 Park Avenue South, Suite 1503,
New York, NY 10016, USA

British Library Cataloguing in Publication Data

Hughes, Martin
    Children and number.
    1. Arithmetic—Study and teaching   2. Number concept
    I. Title
     372.7'2   QA141.15

    ISBN 0-631-13579-0
    ISBN 0-631-13581-2 Pbk

Library of Congress Cataloging in Publication Data

Hughes, Martin.
    Children and number.

    Bibliography: p.
    Includes index.
    1. Number concept in children.   I. Title.
BF723.N8H84   1986   372.7'2   85-26702
ISBN 0-631-13579-0
ISBN 0-631-13581-2 (pbk.)

Typeset by Finlandia Press, Gerrards Cross, Buckinghamshire
Printed in Great Britain by Billings Ltd, Worcester

Contents

Foreword
Margaret Donaldson   vi

Introduction   viii

1 What is the problem?   1

2 Piaget under attack   12

3 Addition and subtraction before school   24

4 What's so hard about two and two?   37

5 Children's invention of written arithmetic   53

6 The written number systems of other cultures   79

7 Understanding the written symbolism of arithmetic   95

8 Children's difficulties in school   113

9 Learning through number games   134

10 Learning with LOGO   152

11 A new approach to number   167

References   185

Index   190

Foreword

Margaret Donaldson

Writing a foreword to *Children and Number* is rather like reviewing a good detective story: one must be careful not to reveal too much of the plot. For the book is full of intriguing puzzles, and it would detract from the reader's interest and satisfaction if these, and the solutions which Martin Hughes offers, were made known before their due place. However, I think it may be justifiable to mention just one of the puzzles so as to convey something of the flavour of the whole.

A central theme in the book is the ability of children to produce and interpret written representations of number. The puzzle I have chosen to reveal is that when children as old as seven – nearly eight – are shown concrete instances of very easy addition and subtraction (two bricks added to a set of two, one brick taken from a set of three and so on) they prove to have very great difficulty in making signs on paper to represent what they have just seen. The difficulty does not lie in representing static numbers of objects (a task that turns out, indeed, to be within the competence of most pre-school children) but rather in representing the changes – the actions of adding and taking away. This in itself is perhaps not particularly surprising. One might expect that changes would be harder to represent than static sets. What is striking, however, is the extent of the differences in difficulty. And what is perplexing, not to say alarming, is to learn that not a single child in a group of ninety-six ever used, or even tried to use, the symbols ' + ' and ' − '. Yet three-quarters of these children were regularly using these symbols when doing addition and subtraction sums in school.

Not one child, then, saw the symbols of the formal arithmetic code as relevant and useful when faced with a problem for which these symbols are precisely appropriate. Why not? How is it that, in spite of all the efforts that have been made to ensure that the teaching of number is well grounded in understanding, this can still be? What have we been overlooking?

As I promised earlier, I shall not anticipate the way in which Hughes deals with this puzzle, or with the others that his studies uncover. I shall merely say that, in a manner characteristic of him, he really does contrive to clear his mind of old assumptions and look afresh at the question of how chidren master "simple arithmetic" – or fail to do so. And then he goes on to make a number of very directly practical suggestions as to how the enterprise of teaching and learning arithmetic may be given a more secure foundation.

No one who reads the book at all seriously and thoughtfully will be left with the impression that this enterprise is ever likely to be an easy one. But on the other hand I believe that most readers will end with the sense of having a better understanding of the true nature of the problem and also with a feeling of encouragement. Hughes does not make extravagant claims for his proposals as to teaching methods. Yet it seems to me that he has succeeded in showing us the start of a highly promising way ahead.

Introduction

This book is about young children's attempts to understand the complex and intriguing world of number. It starts by describing some hitherto unsuspected abilities which children possess before they go to school, such as being able to understand what happens when small quantities of bricks are added to or taken from each other. These early abilities are then contrasted with the difficulties which many children experience when faced with the more formal mathematics of school (as in expressions like 'Three and four makes seven' or '3 + 4 = 7'), and the nature and source of these difficulties is looked at in some detail. Finally, the book outlines some new approaches which teachers and parents might use to help young children acquire a better understanding of number. These range from simple number games, which can be played with everyday objects, to an early use of the computer language LOGO to control the floor-crawling Turtle robot.

The research on which the book is based grew out of my personal dissatisfaction with many widely held assumptions about the capabilities of young children, and particularly with the theories of Jean Piaget. In the early 1970s I was part of a research group in Edinburgh which looked critically at many of Piaget's claims. This research – much of which is summarised in Margaret Donaldson's *Children's Minds* – demonstrated that young children were frequently more competent than Piaget had maintained, particularly if they were studied in contexts that made sense to them, such as when playing simple games. These findings received further support from a study on which I subsequently worked with Barbara Tizard in London (Tizard and Hughes, 1984). In this study we looked at a group of 4-year-old children at home and at nursery school. Again we were impressed by the intellectual capacities of young children, most notably when they were struggling to make sense of their world or when they were playing games.

One episode which we observed made a particularly strong impression on me. It involved a game of knock-out whist between June, a working-class girl of average ability, and her mother. Knock-out whist is a simple card game in which the players take turns to put down cards, with the highest card winning the trick. The players then count up the number of tricks to see who has won each round. The game played by June and her mother was fast and furious, and required the constant use of many numerical skills: indeed, we found it hard to imagine an activity within the scope of a 4-year-old which could pack so much mathematics into so short a time.

June's game of knock-out whist was played at a time when increasing public concern was being voiced about the way in which children are taught mathematics in school. The issues raised by this public debate are important (they are reviewed in chapter 1), and they convinced me of the need for a fresh and more detailed look at how children learn about number. I felt that this enquiry should begin with very young children (those who have not yet started school), and should include a critical scrutiny of assumptions about what they can do and how they learn. I therefore returned to Edinburgh to carry out the research described in this book.

As intended, I initially focused on pre-school children, and on charting the knowledge they acquire informally before starting school. Inevitably, this led me to contrast their natural and informal acquisition of knowledge about number with the difficulties they later encounter in learning the more formal mathematics of school. School mathematics, I felt, should be based on and linked to the understanding of number which children possess when they start school, but my research suggested that these links were not being made. Instead, a serious gap was opening up.

I was not satisfied, however, with merely documenting what was going on: I wanted to find out what could be done to help. My first attempts, inspired by June's example, consisted of simple number games involving everyday objects such as small containers, bricks and dice. These games (which are described in chapter 9) were originally designed for pre-school children, but can easily be extended for older children. Later I looked at a different approach: micro-computers were arriving in schools, and I became interested in how they might be used to help children's mathematical understanding. I was particularly attracted by the computer language LOGO, which allows children to write simple programs themselves. Together, my colleague Hamish Macleod and I produced a simplified version of LOGO for work with pre-school and infant-school children, and the success of this method is described in chapter 10.

I am aware that many people who read this book will have strong negative feelings about number: for them, terms such as 'mathematics' and 'arithmetic' will bring back unpleasant memories of tedious and pointless exercises carried out at school. Some may even argue that mathematics is totally alien to the minds of young children, and that our main concern should be not with introducing it to them but with keeping it away from them for as long as possible. There will also be those who have similarly negative feelings about computers, and who regard them as incomprehensible and alienating machines, with little relevance to the education of young children.

It is not hard to understand why so many people have strong negative feelings about mathematics, given the limitations of our education system. It is also understandable that many people are suspicious of computers, given the frightening uses to which technology is already put in our world. I am certainly not advocating that young children should be pushed at all costs into the worlds of mathematics and technology – indeed many of the problems identified in this book seem to arise from precisely that kind of pressure. At the same time, I have become increasingly impressed by young children's natural abilities to think about and use number, and believe that these abilities should be given much greater recognition than they are at present. The fundamental question is how we can build on the talents and interests that children possess when they first start school, and so reduce the large number of children who leave school lacking both comprehension and interest in mathematics.

Acknowledgements

The research described here was supported initially by a Research Fellowship in Early Childhood Education from the Social Science Research Council, and subsequently by research grants from the Nuffield Foundation and the Scottish Education Department: I am very grateful for this support. My research has also benefited enormously from the direct involvement of Colin Brydon, Miranda Jones, Hamish Macleod, Cathie Potts and Anna Stallard. I am extremely grateful to Ann Brackenridge, Margaret Donaldson, Alison Elliot, Paul Ernest, Jim Hurford, Isobel Hutchings, Miranda Jones, David Pimm and Marilyn Ross for their comments on an earlier draft of the book; to Richard Cowan, Bob Grieve, Jim Howe, Chris Pratt, Peter Ross, Anthony Tomei and Valerie Walkerdine for their advice and encouragement at other times; to Jean Fife for typing the manuscript; to Jessica Rudman for her patient proof-reading; to my editor Philip Carpenter for his advice and for his patience as deadlines came and went; and to the many young children without whom the research could not have taken place. Finally, I am particularly grateful to Ann Brackenridge for her painstaking and invaluable help during the production of the manuscript, and to Margaret Donaldson for her inspiration throughout this work.

I would like to thank the following for permission to reproduce figures: Fontana (2.1), Heinemann Educational Books Ltd (11.3), Jossey-Bass Inc. (6.2), Lawrence Erlbaum Associates Inc. (11.4), John Mason (11.2), W. W. Norton and Co. Inc. (2.1), A. D. Peters and Co. Ltd (6.1, 6.3), *Visible Language* (11.2).

1

What is the problem?

The last few years have seen intense public debate and concern, both in Britain and abroad, about the teaching of mathematics in school. It has been claimed, amongst other things, that standards of numeracy are generally inadequate, that 'progressive' methods in primary schools have failed, that teachers themselves do not know enough mathematics, and that employers are having to provide remedial training in basic skills for their young employees. Many have argued that the solution to these problems lies in the wide-scale assessment of basic skills, and a return to more traditional methods of teaching.

The debate has been further complicated by the sudden and rapid advances in micro-electronics, which have resulted in the widespread availability of first pocket-calculators and then micro-computers. The fact that calculators are now widely used to carry out basic calculations has led to claims that much of the mathematics currently taught in schools has been rendered obsolete, and that children should instead be learning how to use calculators from their very first days in school. Others have argued that, on the contrary, calculators should be kept well away from children, so that they can learn how to carry out mathematical calculations without electronic aid. The debate over computers has taken a slightly different form. Most people seem in favour of using computers in school, but disagree over whether computers should be used as a teaching machine to reinforce basic skills, or as a learning tool to encourage mathematical exploration.

These issues are clearly of crucial importance for all those concerned with – and about – the education of children. They are also directly relevant to any attempt to understand how children learn about number. If we want to know more about the learning process, and particularly about why it is going wrong, then we need to know what mathematical abilities are expected of children by society, and how society is currently attempting to impart these abilities. Our task will obviously be that much harder if there is discord and disagreement about the aims and methods of mathematics education. In fact, as we shall see in this chapter, the intense public debate and interest has led to a much clearer picture of what the fundamental problems might be.

The Cockroft report: *Mathematics Counts*

In Britain, one of the most important contributions to the debate has been the report of a Committee of Inquiry into the Teaching of Mathematics in Schools, under the chairmanship of Dr W. H. Cockroft. This committee was set up in 1978 as a direct response to the widespread public concern about mathematics education, and was composed of mathematicians, mathematics educators, teachers and lay members. Its report, published in 1982, was entitled *Mathematics Counts* but is almost invariably referred to as 'the Cockroft report'. Unlike many official reports, it makes fascinating reading.

Much of the first part of the Cockroft report is concerned with de-bunking some of the claims being made about deficiencies in children's mathematical skills. For example, the committee investigated the extent of employers' dissatisfaction with the mathematical understanding of school-leavers. It reported (para. 46) that the overall picture was much more encouraging than the earlier complaints had led them to expect, and found little real dissatisfaction amongst employers with the mathematical capabilities of those whom they recruited from schools. The report also quoted from a study of 300 employers in England and Wales by Professor Gareth Williams of Lancaster University. This study found that only 14 per cent of employers criticised the educational standards of their recruits: more common criticisms were of 'inability to take work seriously, lack of interest, unwillingness to work, bad time-keeping and poor attendance' (para. 48).

The committee found little evidence that standards of numeracy were declining, although it accepted that it was not easy to compare one era with another. It did, however, point out that similar criticisms concerning the teaching of mathematics had been made at frequent intervals dating back to 1876 at least. This observation not only puts current criticisms in perspective but also, more importantly, indicates that children's difficulties with mathematics are by no means a passing phenomenon.

The Cockroft committee was not, however, complacent about the existing state of affairs. It reported with some concern that many children leave school with negative attitudes towards mathematics, and that many adults have deeply rooted feelings of anxiety and inadequacy about the subject. A research team commissioned by the committee attempted to interview a sample of adults on the mathematics they used in everyday life, but found that half of those approached refused to be interviewed simply because the subject was mathematics. Another study, carried out by the Advisory Council for Adult and Continuing Education in conjunction with the Gallup Poll, reported (para. 20) that 'The extent to which the need to undertake even an apparently simple and straight-forward piece of mathematics could induce feelings of anxiety, helpless-ness, fear and even guilt in some of those interviewed was, perhaps, the most striking feature of the study.' These researchers also found that many adults, whilst being able to perform mathematical calcula-tions, felt inadequate because they knew they were not using the 'proper' methods which they had been taught at school. Other adults used different strategies for coping with the mathematical demands of everyday life – such as always buying £10-worth of petrol, or paying by cheque, so as to avoid the need to calculate the change.

A central theme of the Cockroft report is that most of the mathematics used in everyday life and at work is embedded in practical problems. In a key paragraph of the report (para. 249), it is argued that the ability to solve problems is at the heart of mathematics:

> Mathematics is only 'useful' to the extent to which it can be applied to a particular situation, and it is the ability to apply mathematics to a variety of situations to which we give the name 'problem-solving'. However, the solution of a mathematical problem cannot begin until the problem has been translated into the appropriate mathematical terms. This first and essential step presents very great difficulties to many pupils – a fact which is often too little appreciated.

The above argument – which is of central importance to this book – formed the basis of several of the Cockroft committee's recommen-dations. The committee argued that there should be less emphasis on basic skills by themselves, and declared (para. 278) that 'The results of a "back-to-basics" approach...are most unlikely to be those which its proponents wish to see, and we can in no way support or recommend an approach of this kind.' Instead, more attention should be given to applying these skills to real situations; there should be much more discussion of mathematical problems in classrooms, both between pupils and teacher and between the pupils themselves; and there should be more practical work and problem-solving. Above all, the committee argued that teachers should be aiming not just to teach concepts and skills, but to help children understand how these concepts can be applied in practical situations, both familiar and unfamiliar.

The same kind of thinking lay behind the report's recommendations on calculators (the timing of the report meant that it had little to say concerning more recent developments with micro-computers). The Cockroft committee argued that, as calculators will be increasingly used in employment and in everyday life, children should be taught how to use them. At the same time, it stressed that using a calculator in no way reduces the need for mathematical understanding on the part of the person using it (para. 378): 'A calculator can be no use until a decision has been made as to the mathematical operation which needs to be carried out and experience shows that children (and also adults) whose mathematical understanding is weak are very often reluctant to make use of a calculator.' In other words, an essential part of real mathematical problem-solving lies in translating the problem into the appropriate mathematical form, and with this the calculator cannot help.

Mathematical understanding in children aged 11 to 13 years

The Cockroft committee's claim that children's failings lie more in the area of problem-solving than in the possession of basic skills is supported by a number of more detailed surveys. For example, the Assessment of Performance Unit (APU), which had been set up in 1975 to monitor the achievements of school children, produced its first report in 1980 on the mathematical performance of 30,000 11-year-olds in England and Wales. This report concluded (p. xv) that 'most [of these children] can do mathematics involving the more fundamental concepts and skills to which they have been introduced and also simple applications of them. There is, however, a fairly sharp decline in performance as pupils' understanding of the concepts is probed more deeply and their basic knowledge has to be applied in more complex settings or unfamiliar contexts.'

A good illustration of this point comes from two questions in the APU survey involving simple division. The first question was a relatively familiar application of division:

A bar of chocolate can be broken into 18 squares. There are 6 squares in each row. How many rows are there?

The survey found that 83 per cent of 11-year-olds could answer this question correctly. However, a very different picture emerged when the children were asked to calculate Geoff Boycott's batting average:

A batting average in cricket is found by dividing the number of runs scored by number of times out. Fill in the following table.

Name	No.times out	No.runs scored	Average
Boycott	5	500	....

Only 25 per cent of the children tested got this one right, despite the fact that the division involved (500 divided by 5) is extremely simple; 38 per cent of the children apparently did not even attempt the question.

This is a very revealing finding. The children are actually given all the information needed to produce a correct answer: they are told how to calculate an average and then given a simple example. Yet, despite this, a large proportion of children were seemingly frightened off, perhaps by the mention of 'averages', or maybe even by the mention of 'cricket' and 'Boycott'. Whatever the reason, many children were, in the words of the Cockroft report, unable to translate the problem into the appropriate mathematical terms, and so failed on a question which should have been well within their means.

Children's difficulties in deriving the relevant mathematical calculation from a real-life problem were highlighted in another survey carried out by a team of researchers from Chelsea College at the University of London (Hart, 1981). Children aged 11 to 13 years were presented with problems like the following:

The Green family have to drive 261 miles to get from London to Leeds. After driving 87 miles, they stop for lunch. How do you work out how far they still have to drive?

$$87 \times 3 \qquad 261 + 87 \qquad 87 \div 261 \qquad 261 - 87$$

$$261 \times 87 \qquad 261 \div 87 \qquad 87 - 261 \qquad 87 + 174$$

Here the children are only required to select a particular calculation and do not have to carry it out. Nevertheless, the researchers found that only 60 per cent of the 12-year-olds selected the correct answer (261 − 87), with a further 19 per cent selecting the inverse calculation (87 − 261). Similar difficulties emerged for all the basic operations of addition, subtraction, multiplication and division.

Some insights into the children's difficulties with this question are given by the following dialogue with Tony (a 13-year-old). His problem was similar to the one above, but involved the numbers 228 and 87.

Tony: You add it on again...you add...three on to make 80 and then
  another 20 to make 100, then 128 from that is eh...one hundred
  and forty something.
Interviewer: Which of these [expressions] do you think...?
Tony: That one [87 + 228].
Interviewer: Are you sure it's that one? Did you add 87 on to 228?
Tony: No, I built it up.
Interviewer: You built it up? Do you think it's any of these [expressions]?
Tony: I think it's this one [87 ÷ 228].
Interviewer: 87 divided by 228?
Tony: No...I don't know the sign for adding it on.

Tony's difficulties arise from the fact that, like many children, he actually
solves subtraction problems by a process of addition. As he himself puts
it, he 'builds up' his answer from the smaller number in the subtraction. This method is typical of the untaught or non-standard methods
referred to in the Cockroft report. While it may often be effective in
obtaining the answer (although it was not in Tony's case), it causes severe
problems when it has to be translated into a standard form.

Mathematical understanding in American children

The public concern with mathematical standards is by no means unique
to Britain: similar debates have been taking place throughout western
Europe, North America and Australia. The United States, for example,
has seen a very similar concern with standards of numeracy and
mathematical understanding in school children. As in Britain, large-scale
surveys have been carried out in order to assess levels of performance
and understanding across the nation.
  In 1973, 1978 and 1982, the National Assessment of Educational
Progress (NAEP) carried out surveys of mathematical understanding
in children aged 9 to 17 years. Over 46,000 children took part in the
1982 survey (NAEP, 1983). The performance of this sample in basic
mathematical skills was as high as or higher than that of previous years:
most children seemed to have the ability to carry out basic mathematical
calculations. As in Britain, however, performance was lower when the
children were asked to solve problems in which the relevant mathematical
calculations had to be extracted from the problem. For example, although

60 per cent of the 13-year-olds could multiply two fractions, only 17 per cent could solve the following problem: 'George had $\frac{3}{4}$ of a pie. He ate $\frac{3}{5}$ of that. How much pie did he eat?'

The children's performance was particularly disappointing on problems which required a careful analysis of the problem and not just a routine calculation. For example, the 13-year-olds in the NAEP survey were given the following problem:

> An army bus holds 36 soldiers. If 1128 soldiers are being bused to their training site, how many buses are needed?

Overall, about 70 per cent of the children performed the correct calculation (that is, they divided 1128 by 36), and most of these produced the correct answer to that calculation: 31.33 (many of these children used calculators). What was particularly revealing, however, was that nearly a third of the pupils proceeded to write this as the answer to the problem (i.e. 31.33 buses), thus ignoring the need for a whole number of buses. A different mistake was made by nearly a quarter of the children who ignored the remainder altogether, thus leaving 12 soldiers with no transport. A clear grasp of the problem would have led to the realisation that the answer had to be rounded *up* to the *next* whole number – assuming, of course, that it was not feasible to squash the extra soldiers into the smaller number of buses.

The NAEP surveys also looked at the ability of American children to carry out estimations. This aspect of mathematical understanding is particularly important if calculators are being used to carry out routine calculations. If pupils estimate in advance a reasonable answer to their problem, then they will have greater confidence if the calculator produces an answer close to their estimate, and they will also be able to spot if a mistake has been made.

In the second NAEP survey, 13-year-olds were asked to estimate the sum of $\frac{12}{13}$ and $\frac{7}{8}$. They were given the following answers to choose from: '1', '2', '19', '21', and 'I don't know'. According to James Hiebert (1984), only 24 per cent chose the correct answer, '2', while 28 per cent chose the answer '19' and 27 per cent chose the answer '21'. As Hiebert himself comments (p. 506): 'The last two answers were obtained by meaningless symbol manipulation – adding the numerators and adding the denominators respectively. Apparently, it did not bother these students that they had added two numbers, each slightly less than one, and had obtained an answer of 19 or 21.'

The failure of progressivism

These recent surveys of British and American children point to some clear but depressing conclusions. Most children aged 11 to 13 years seem able to perform calculations involving the four basic arithmetical operations of addition, subtraction, multiplication and division. However, their understanding of these calculations frequently appears to be limited, and in many cases their performance consists entirely of the meaningless manipulation of symbols. Furthermore, their ability to apply these basic operations to new and unfamiliar problems seems severely restricted.

Such findings provide little support for those who believe that basic skills are being neglected in primary or elementary schools, and that all that is needed is a widespread 'return to basics'. At the same time, the conclusions reached will surprise many who believe that this problem was solved by the introduction of 'progressive' methods into British primary schools in the 1950s and 1960s. Surely, it will be argued, the progressive movement had as its ultimate goal the replacement of methods based on drill and rote-learning with those based on discovery and understanding? And, if so, why has this not been achieved?

There is little doubt that the principles and methods which are loosely labelled 'progressive' have always put understanding to the fore. An important early document in the British progressive movement was the Mathematical Association's report in 1956 called *The Teaching of Mathematics in Primary Schools*. This report argued (p. 17) that:

> ...understanding must precede drill or formal exercises intended to develop memory, mechanical accuracy or speed....It is not because we under-estimate the value of accuracy and the orderly arrangement of computation that we have given comparatively little emphasis to the written arithmetic which is traditional in classroom practice and in textbooks. Rather, it is because we are convinced that the important thing is to help children to understand mathematical ideas and to recognise the kind of computation or other thought processes which a problem situation demands.

Similar ideas lay behind several curriculum innovations proposed in the 1960s, with their emphasis on practical activities and discovery methods: a classic example is the Nuffield Primary Mathematics Project with its motto 'I do and I understand'. The same message has since been put forward in a wide range of documents and guidelines for primary teachers, such as *Mathematics 5–11* by Her Majesty's Inspectorate (DES

1979), and in countless in-service courses for teachers throughout Britain. Yet, as Hilary Shuard (1984) points out (p. 587):

> The central issue in primary mathematics raised by Cockroft is why, nearly 30 years after the impetus for broadening the primary mathematics curriculum began and after so much official support has been given to a broad primary mathematics curriculum that emphasizes understanding, practical work, and discovery, it was still necessary for the Cockroft report to repeat the same message in a way that suggested that it had not yet been fully understood or carried out in practice in most primary schools.

Indeed, it seems clear from several recent studies that progressive ideas have made little headway in British primary schools. For example, a survey by Her Majesty's Inspectorate of 80 first schools (5 to 9 years: DES 1982), discovered that in only one-fifth of the schools was there 'a good balance between learning how to perform a calculation and using it in a practical setting'. In the remaining four-fifths a good balance was not achieved, and skills were usually practised in isolation from practical problems. The survey noted that written calculations often formed the main element in mathematics work, and in some schools the sole aim seemed to be for the children to reach a standard of efficiency in abstract calculations.

These findings are supported by a more detailed study by Neville Bennett and his colleagues (1984) of the quality of the learning environments provided by sixteen able teachers of children aged 6 to 7 years. On the subject of mathematics, this study concluded (p. 97) that 'Even the most successful class in which a wide curriculum, brisk pacing and attention to progress and consolidation were evident, was marked by the lack of attention to genuine practical relevance in the maths experience provided.'

Similar findings were reported in a study of British junior schools (8 to 11 years) published in late 1984, which received much attention from the British national press. The study, carried out by Joan Barker-Lunn of the National Foundation for Educational Research, was based on questionnaire responses from over 2000 junior school teachers. In the area of mathematics, 82 per cent of the teachers responded that they placed foremost emphasis on basic computational skills – learning multiplication tables and number bonds. Barker-Lunn concluded (p. 187) that there is no need to exhort the vast majority of junior school teachers to go back to the basics: 'Indeed the development of and practice in the basic skills of English and of mathematics would seem to be the predominant features of junior school classrooms.'

Several reasons have been put forward to explain why progressivism has failed to produce the impact which its advocates once hoped for. The most common ones are: pressure from parents and from secondary schools for more visible evidence of mathematical progress, such as the ability to carry out written calculations; teachers' own lack of confidence and understanding of progressive methods; and the large amount of extra work required from teachers using these methods. Critics of progressivism have also argued that some of the ideas involved (such as sets and matrices) are not easy for children to grasp, while other critics have argued that too much emphasis was placed on understanding at the expense of calculation: as the jibe has it, children using progressive methods know that '3 + 4' is the same as '4 + 3', but do not know that both these add up to seven.

There may also be a further factor which has not received so much attention. The main theoretical underpinning for progressivism has always come from the work of the great Swiss psychologist and epistemologist Jean Piaget, and advocates of progressivism make frequent references to him in their writings. As we shall see in the next chapter, however, Piaget's ideas have in recent years been subject to increasing criticism: this in turn suggests that some of the assumptions underlying progressivism are due for reappraisal.

Overview

Recent findings from both Britain and America point to three related conclusions. First, it is becoming widely recognised that proficiency in the basic skills of numeracy is not enough: what is needed is the ability to apply these skills to real-life practical problems. The increasing use of calculators emphasises rather than diminishes the need to understand what calculations are required, to make a reasonable estimate of the answer, and to think carefully about the implications of the answer. Secondly, it appears that large numbers of children leave primary or elementary school without this wider mathematical understanding: while children's performance of basic calculations is superficially adequate, their understanding of these calculations, their ability to apply their skills to new problems, and their ability to interpret their findings are frequently inadequate. Finally, despite popular belief to the contrary, most British primary schools are not paying sufficient attention to developing this wider mathematical understanding and are in fact placing *too much* emphasis on basic computational skills.

These conclusions in turn indicate three major areas where we need to increase our understanding. First, we need to find out precisely what is involved in applying mathematical skills to practical situations. Secondly, we need to find out why this kind of mathematical understanding is so difficult for so many children. And, finally, we need to know what methods can be used to help children attain this wider mathematical understanding.

Much of this book is concerned with providing some initial answers to these questions. As the research on which it is based grew out of my dissatisfaction with the theories of Jean Piaget, it is relevant to look first at Piaget's theories – and at the criticisms recently made of them – in order to understand why an alternative account is needed.

2

Piaget under attack

For some time now Jean Piaget has been regarded as one of the leading authorities on the question of how children learn mathematics. This position is well justified, as he has given us many important insights into young children's understanding of mathematical concepts. In recent years, however, several aspects of Piaget's theory – including those concerned with children's early understanding of number – have received serious criticism from psychologists in both Britain and America. These criticisms are of considerable importance and worth looking at carefully. First, though, I will sketch out the main characteristics of Piaget's theory and look at what he has to say about the way children learn mathematics.

Piaget's theory of intellectual development

In trying to understand Piaget's impact on mathematics education, we are faced straight away with a puzzle. Despite his undoubted influence, Piaget in fact devoted very little of his writings to the question of how children learn mathematics, and even less to the question of how they might be helped in school. He was indeed a prolific writer and it is estimated that, in the course of his lifetime, he and his co-workers produced over 1500 books and articles on psychology and epistemology (the theory of knowledge). However, only a very small number of these publications are explicitly concerned with the problems of learning mathematics.

To account for this puzzle, two important features of Piaget's work must be recognised. First, as Piaget himself repeatedly claimed throughout his life, his primary interest was in epistemology rather than psychology: he wanted, above all, to understand how knowledge in general is gained and enlarged by the human race, rather than how particular pieces of knowledge are gained by particular individuals.

Nevertheless, he appreciated that studies of the general and of the particular must go hand in hand, and he was always searching for links or parallels between the way individual knowledge progresses and the way more general knowledge progresses.

The second important feature of Piaget's work which must be recognised is this: just as his interest in the psychological development of the child was in many ways secondary to his epistemological interest, so his interest in the child's understanding of mathematics was in many ways secondary to his interest in the child's more general psychological development. Over the years, Piaget developed a highly intricate theory to explain the development of thinking and understanding in children from birth to adulthood, and insights into the growth of mathematical thinking came as a result of this more general theory rather than the other way round. The importance of this point – and the previous one – will become apparent later when we look at criticisms of Piaget's theory.

The theory itself is too complex to have full justice done to it here. A succinct summary of some of Piaget's main ideas is provided in the appendix of Donaldson (1978), while a more detailed review is provided by Flavell (1963). Here we will look at one aspect of Piaget's theory, the idea of *stages of development*, and focus in detail on two crucial tasks which he used to support his theory.

Of central theoretical importance to Piaget is the notion that there are discrete stages of development, each with its own properties and characteristics, through which all children must pass in a prescribed order between birth and adulthood. According to Piaget, the child's capacities for learning and understanding – and indeed the whole way the child sees the world – are very much determined by their particular stage of development.

The first main stage in Piaget's theory is called the *sensori-motor period*, and covers the time from birth to about 18 months (these stages are only loosely tied to particular ages). One of the main achievements made by infants in this period is the realisation that they are separate from the rest of the world, and that there is a world of objects which is independent of their own actions. An important discovery of Piaget's was that a baby aged less than 6 months appears not to realise that objects continue to exist when they are no longer visible: the baby will therefore not reach for objects which are hidden by a cloth.

The second stage of development, covering the period from roughly 18 months to 7 years, is known as the *pre-operational period*. For Piaget, this long period, during which many developments are taking place in the young child, is unified by the *lack* of many features which emerge in the next stage of development. According to Piaget, pre-operational children are dominated by their perceptions, and so are likely to be misled by what they see: for example, they appear to think that the volume of a liquid changes as it is poured from one container into another of different size or shape. He also claimed that they are egocentric, in the sense of being unable to take another person's point of view, and that they do not understand simple logical inferences.

The pre-operational stage is followed at around 7 years by the *concrete operational period*. The main characteristic here is that the child is able to think logically about operations performed in the physical world: the child's thinking has become decentred and capable of many logical inferences. Children of this stage are aware that certain changes in the physical world can be reversed, and realise the implications of this: they now appreciate, for example, that the volume of liquid remains unchanged by its transfer from one container to another.

The final stage of development is known as the *formal operational period*. This stage, which usually manifests itself at around 11 years or later, is characterised by the possession of full logical thinking. The child is now able to think logically, not only about the physical world, but also about the world of hypothetical statements. The child can reason about possibilities and hypotheses: at this stage the deductive reasoning characteristic of science becomes possible.

The evidence which Piaget puts forward to support his theory comes from a large number of ingenious experiments devised by his co-workers and himself. The main characteristic of these experiments is that the adult presents the child with a task or problem, and then diagnoses the child's state of development from their comments and reasoning. Two of the tasks which Piaget used to study the transition from pre-operational to concrete operational thinking are concerned explicitly with number. These two problems – of class-inclusion and conservation – not only are of central importance to Piaget's views on early mathematics education, but also have become the focus of much recent criticism. For both these reasons they are worth looking at in detail.

Class-inclusion and conservation

The class-inclusion problem is intended to be a test of the child's ability to compare a set with a subset of itself – or a whole with a part of that whole. In a typical version of the problem the child is presented with a collection of wooden beads, most of which are brown but some of which are white. The child is asked: 'Are there more brown beads or wooden beads?' Piaget found that children aged 6 years or under generally reply to this question that there are more brown beads. They appear to be comparing, not part with whole, but one of the parts with the other. It is only when they reach the age of around 7 years that children will consistently answer 'More wooden beads'.

Piaget argued that the performance of pre-operational children on the class-inclusion problem is strong evidence of their intellectual limitations. His argument, in brief, was that the pre-operational child is simply incapable of comparing a set with one of its subsets. According to Piaget, the child can attend either to the set or to the subset, but can never take account of both at the same time.

While the class-inclusion task is primarily about the child's logical capacities it is also, according to Piaget, relevant to their understanding of number. In *The Child's Conception of Number* (1952), Piaget claims that understanding class-inclusion is an essential prerequisite for understanding addition and subtraction. He argues (p. 190) that children may appear to understand the words 'Two and six makes eight', but will not understand what this means until they understand how the set 'eight' can be broken down into its subsets 'two' and 'six', and then reconstituted again. Thus, according to Piaget, young children cannot really understand addition and subtraction until they solve the class-inclusion problem at around 7 years.

The second task which is crucial to Piaget's account of early mathematical thinking concerns the conservation of number. In a typical version of the standard number-conservation task the child is first shown two rows of counters. Usually these rows contain the same number of counters, and they are placed in one-to-one correspondence as shown below:

O O O O O O
X X X X X X

The child is asked if there are the same number of counters in each row: if the child agrees that there are, then the test can proceed. One row of counters is now displaced so that the two rows are no longer of the same length, but the overall number of counters in each row remains the same (see below). The displacement is usually pointed out to the child by the adult saying something like 'Now watch what I do.'

O O O O O O
X   X   X   X   X   X

The adult now repeats the original question, asking the child again if there are the same number of counters in each row. If the child still agrees that the two rows contain the same number, then the child is said to have 'conserved' number. Otherwise, the child is said to be a 'non-conserver'.

Piaget found that children below the age of 7 years commonly do not conserve number. That is, they respond as if they believe that changing the length of the row changes its numerosity. On the other hand, children over the age of 7 years usually agree that the rows still contain the same number of counters despite the change in length: their judgement of number appears unaffected by this change.

Piaget's conservation tasks have received a vast amount of careful scrutiny from developmental psychologists all over the world. As we shall see later, many of them do not now accept Piaget's conclusions. Nevertheless, the notion of conservation has been particularly influential within early mathematics education, and it has been used by many teachers as a yardstick of progress in children's early mathematical development.

Piaget and mathematics education

In addition to his 'stage' theory of development, Piaget also had distinctive views on the way in which mathematics is learnt – and therefore on how it should be taught. Much of Piaget's writing is dense with his own terminology and difficult to understand, but one important exception is an article which appeared in *Scientific American* in 1953, in which his ideas on mathematics education are put forward with unusual clarity. The first two paragraphs (p. 74) are worth quoting in full:

It is a great mistake to suppose that a child acquires the notion of number and other mathematical concepts just from teaching. On the contrary, to a remarkable degree he develops them himself, independently and spontaneously. When adults try to impose mathematical concepts on a child prematurely, his learning is merely verbal; true understanding of them comes only with his mental growth.

This can easily be shown by a simple experiment. A child of five or six may readily be taught by his parents to name the numbers from 1 to 10. If 10 stones are laid in a row, he can count them correctly. But if the stones are rearranged in a more complex pattern or piled up, he no longer can count them with consistent accuracy. Although the child knows the names of the numbers, he has not yet grasped the essential idea of number: namely, that the number of objects in a group remains the same, is 'conserved', no matter how they are shuffled or arranged.

These paragraphs contain several characteristically Piagetian ideas. Thus we find here the interrelated beliefs that teaching children before they are conceptually 'ready' can produce only superficial learning, that true learning comes only with the child's mental growth, and that to a large extent mathematical concepts cannot be taught. There is, too, the implication that learning mathematics is not essentially difficult, for it is something which children will for the most part do 'independently and spontaneously'. Central importance is also given here to the idea of conservation: Piaget maintains that if children cannot conserve number then they are not yet ready to start on school arithmetic. Indeed, Piaget suggests that teachers should mistrust any apparent ability – such as counting – that young children bring with them to school: if the children cannot conserve then this apparent knowledge is likely to be merely parrot-style learning.

Many of these ideas of Piaget's were repeated in another short article he wrote almost 20 years later, *Comments on Mathematical Education* (1973). Here he reiterated his belief that learning mathematics could not take place simply by the teacher transmitting knowledge to the learner, and again argued that the building up of mathematical knowledge came about as a natural result of the more general growth of the child's logical capabilities. He emphasised (p. 85) that this 'natural' method of learning took place through the child's activities and through discovery: 'Real comprehension of a notion or a theory implies the reinvention of this theory by the subject.'

Piaget never spelt out in detail how these ideas should be put into practice in the classroom. Nevertheless, he has usually been interpreted as advocating a very late introduction to formal symbolism, with a corresponding earlier emphasis on children's engaging in physical activities with materials such as sand, water, buttons, beads and bricks. It is assumed that pouring water from one container into another, or sorting objects into sets, will help develop children's mathematical concepts, and that they will proceed to formalisation only when they are conceptually ready. For many followers of Piaget, the teacher's role is regarded as being intellectually non-interventionist and relatively un-important: mathematics is essentially contructed by the children themselves.

It is interesting to compare Piaget's ideas with the earlier and very different theoretical approach of the American behaviourist Edward Thorndike. According to Thorndike (1922), learning arithmetic is essentially a process of forming bonds between a stimulus (e.g. 'two and two') and a response ('four'). As with other aspects of behaviourist theory, practice followed by reward is considered the most likely mechanism by which the bonding would take place. Children would thus be required to repeat statements such as 'Two and two makes four' until they knew them by heart. Such a theory takes little account of the child's level of conceptual development: all that is required is the possibility that such bonds can be formed in the child's brain. As Thorndike declared (p. xi):

> The aims of elementary education, when fully defined, will be found to be the production of changes in human nature represented by an almost countless list of connections or bonds whereby the pupil thinks or feels or acts in certain ways in response to the situations the school has organised and is influenced to think and feel and act similarly to similar situations when life outside of school confronts him with them.

It is easy to see how appealing Piaget's theories might be to educators dissatisfied with traditional methods such as those advocated by Thorndike. In particular, Piaget's view of the active part which children themselves play in constructing their own knowledge, together with the need to take account of the level and nature of their own conceptual structures, makes a sharp contrast with the theories of behaviourists such as Thorndike. Piaget's theories have thus been extensively invoked by progressivists and others attempting to develop new approaches to mathematics based on discovery and activity.

In Britain today Piaget's ideas are still influential, particularly amongst those working with nursery children (3 to 5 years) and reception-class children (5 to 6 years). It is generally considered, for example, that 'Piagetian' activities involving the physical manipulation of concrete objects – such as matching objects on a one-to-one basis and sorting them into sets – constitute appropriate mathematical activities for these young children. Beyond this age, Piaget's influence rapidly diminishes: as we have already seen, there is a widespread reluctance in British primary schools to use activity- and discovery-methods, and instead a concentration on the basics of formal arithmetic. The same appears to be true in the United States and elsewhere. Indeed, it is fair to say that at present truly Piagetian classrooms are few and far between.

Critical research on Piaget's number tasks

For some years now psychologists, both in Britain and abroad, have
been reporting findings which cast doubt on aspects of Piaget's theory
(e.g. Bryant, 1974; Donaldson, 1978; Gelman and Gallistel, 1978). Much
of this research has focused on the tasks which Piaget used to assess
children's stage of development. Many psychologists share the belief
that children's failure on some of these tasks might be due to factors
other than lack of ability. In particular, it is felt that Piaget's tasks
frequently do not make sufficiently clear what the children are supposed
to do.

The two tasks described earlier – class-inclusion and conservation –
have been amongst those receiving this kind of attention. Several studies
have now been carried out which suggest that young children can, under
certain circumstances, succeed on these tasks. Two particularly elegant
studies were carried out by James McGarrigle, a fellow student of mine
in Edinburgh in the 1970s.

McGarrigle first looked at the class-inclusion task. He did not dispute
Piaget's claim that children below 7 years typically respond to this task
by comparing the two subsets (in the example given earlier, the brown
beads with the white beads) rather than, as requested, the subset with
the whole set (the brown beads with the wooden beads). McGarrigle
was, however, critical of Piaget's explanation that young children do
this because they lack the conceptual ability to do otherwise. Instead,
he believed that children misinterpret the problem and therefore carry
out a task different from that intended.

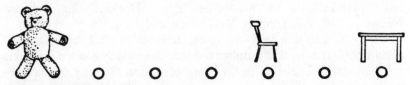

Figure 2:1   Teddy's steps
(from Donaldson, 1978, p. 45 copyright © 1978 by Margaret Donaldson. By
permission of W. W. Norton and Co. Inc.)

McGarrigle devised a number of experiments to distinguish between
these two explanations. One of them involved a teddy bear, a set of flat
counters, a teddy-size chair and a teddy-size table. These were laid out
so that there were four counters leading from the teddy to the chair,
and a further two counters from the chair to the table (see figure 2.1).

McGarrigle told the children that the counters were 'steps' along which the teddy travelled, either to his chair or to his table. He then asked the children questions very similar to the class-inclusion question – for example, 'Are there more steps to go to the chair or more steps to go to the table?' McGarrigle found that over two-thirds of a group of children aged 3 to 5 years answered this question correctly – a far higher percentage than that normally found with standard class-inclusion tasks. McGarrigle concluded that the child's interpretation of the task is of paramount importance in determining their performance (for more details see McGarrigle, Grieve and Hughes, 1978).

This point was brought out even more strikingly in another study which McGarrigle carried out, this time with Margaret Donaldson (McGarrigle and Donaldson, 1974). Their study focused on Piaget's number-conservation task. It will be recalled that in the original version of the task the child first agrees that two rows of counters arranged in one-to-one correspondence contain the same number of counters. The adult then deliberately rearranges the array and repeats the question. It seemed to McGarrigle and Donaldson, however, that this deliberate rearrangement might signal to children that something of importance had changed, and that they should therefore alter their response.

McGarrigle and Donaldson devised an alternative means of presentation in which the transformation of the array was apparently carried out accidentally. This was done by invoking the services of a 'Naughty Teddy' – actually manipulated by the adult – who emerged from a box and messed up the game. A systematic study showed that significantly more children conserved number when the transformation was carried out 'accidentally' by Naughty Teddy than with the standard presentation of the task, thus supporting McGarrigle and Donaldson's explanation rather than Piaget's. Further studies (e.g. by Dockrell, Campbell and Neilson, 1980) also support McGarrigle and Donaldson's claim.

More evidence that very young children understand the invariance of number – that is, that number does not necessarily change if objects are displaced – comes from the work of Rochel Gelman and her co-workers in America (Gelman and Gallistel, 1978). Much of Gelman's evidence comes from studies using her ingenious 'magic' game. In this game children develop an expectancy that a particular array will contain, for example, three objects. The array is then surreptitiously ('magically') altered in one of two ways. In one condition the objects are simply rearranged, while in the second condition objects are added to or taken from the array. In both cases the reaction of the children to the change in the array is carefully noted. On the basis of these studies, Gelman claims that children as young as 3 years understand the invariance of small numbers – that is when there are three objects or fewer on display. They appear to understand that displacing the objects in such an array does not affect its numerosity in the way that adding or subtracting objects does.

The studies just described show that children in Piaget's 'preoperational' stage are much more competent with number than he allows for. This has serious implications for Piaget's views on early mathematics education which, as we have seen, rest heavily on the belief that preoperational children have an inadequate concept of number. However, these studies tell us more than that. In particular, it has been argued by Donaldson (1978) that they demonstrate an important property of children's thinking.

Embedded and disembedded thinking

Donaldson argues that both the Piagetian tasks discussed here – class-inclusion and conservation – involve language in a particular way. In order to succeed on them, children have to attend closely to the language used by the adult. In both tasks, the problem actually posed by the adult does not accord with the child's natural interpretation of the situation. Thus, in the class-inclusion task, children will tend to focus on the perceptually salient differences between the sub-groups, while the wording of the problem requires them to focus on the distinction between sub-group and overall group. Similarly, in the conservation task, the adult's actions suggest that one interpretation of the problem is appropriate, while their actual question requires that a different interpretation be made.

Donaldson claims that both these problems require what she calls 'disembedded' thinking: the child must think about the language used by the adult independently from the context in which it is being used. The child must attend to the words in themselves. This, she argues, is extremely difficult, not only for young children but also for older children and adults. According to Donaldson, thinking which is embedded in a context which makes sense comes relatively easily. 'However, when we move beyond the bounds of human sense there is a dramatic difference' (p. 76).

Many of Donaldson's ideas are relevant to the problems of learning mathematics. As we shall see in chapter 4, a crucial feature of much of the mathematics learnt in school is that it is relatively 'disembedded' from the immediate context. In contrast to Piaget, Donaldson's account would thus predict that children will have considerable difficulty in learning mathematics *whenever it is taught to them*.

Is Piaget relevant?

There is a further criticism that can be made of Piaget's theory. It has been argued, not that his theory is incorrect, but that it lacks immediate relevance for those attempting to cope with children's real difficulties in learning mathematics. Piaget's theory, in other words, is able neither to predict the kind of difficulties seen in chapter 1, nor to offer much specific advice on how to cope with them. Indeed, one can easily interpret him as saying that learning mathematics is not an essentially difficult business, since he sees mathematical concepts as arising to a large degree 'independently and spontaneously'.

One version of this criticism is that Piaget's ideas are simply too complex and in many places too obscure to be useful. It has often been argued, albeit somewhat jokingly, that his theory can never be disproved, as he can always use one part of his theory to explain any evidence which casts doubt on another part. As Guy Groen and Carolyn Kieran (1983) point out (p. 352): '...Piaget's theory is so subtle, ambiguous and open to misinterpretation...that it has simply been abandoned for a more manageable framework.'

Groen and Kieran also make the point that the tasks which Piaget developed to study children's thinking – and even those tasks specifically concerned with number – may not be particularly relevant for understanding the difficulties they face when confronted with school mathematics. Indeed, Piaget himself as good as admits this when he argues that conservation and class-inclusion are primarily not mathematical ideas, but logical ideas. As Groen and Kieran point out (op. cit. p. 360), 'conservation and reversibility originate in epistemological rather than psychological notions. They grew out of formal considerations of the structure of knowledge, rather than some theory of children's thinking.' The implication is that we will gain a better understanding of why children find school mathematics difficult if we look at how they perform on problems which more closely resemble the problems they face in school.

Overview

Piaget's views on education embody admirable general principles about the need for children to understand what they are learning in their own terms. Few would want to question this aspect of Piaget's theory. However, his theory has come in for some more serious criticisms: it is claimed that he has underestimated young children's abilities, that he has ignored the context in which thinking takes place (and in particular the relationship between the context and the language of his tasks), and that his views on education, while attractive, are not relevant to understanding the difficulties which children experience in learning school mathematics.

These criticisms of Piaget not only suggest that a fresh approach is neccessary, but also give us some clues as to where to start. They suggest we should take a new look at the abilities children possess *before they start school*, for it is pre-school children who have been most seriously underestimated. They also suggest we should move away from the traditional Piagetian tasks of class-inclusion and conservation, and look instead at abilities which are more closely related to the kind of mathematics children learn in school. Finally, they suggest that we should devise tasks which make sense to young children, so that we can look at their strengths rather than their weaknesses, at what they *can* do rather than at what they *cannot*. If we can get a clearer picture of what children actually know about number when they first come to school, we should be one step nearer to understanding what is subsequently going wrong.

3

Addition and subtraction before school

In developing a new approach to number, a good place to start is with the fundamental mathematical activities of adding and subtracting. Unlike many of the abilities studied by Piaget, addition and subtraction are directly involved in most aspects of school mathematics. They also underlie many calculations in everyday life – such as adding up a bill, working out change and checking that one has been paid correctly. Even if we rely increasingly on calculators to carry out these calculations, we will still need to understand the underlying mathematical operations.

Despite their importance, addition and subtraction hardly feature in Piaget's theory. When he did devote some attention to them, his main concern was to demonstrate their relationship to his fundamental concepts of class-inclusion and conservation. Thus he argued (e.g. Piaget, 1952) that true understanding of addition and subtraction cannot be attained before the onset of concrete operational thinking at around 7 years. As we have seen, he admitted that younger children can sometimes be taught to repeat certain formulae, such as 'Two and four makes six', but argued that this cannot be considered as true understanding without the abilities to conserve the number six and to understand how it can be broken down into its constituent parts and then reconstituted again.

Piaget is not alone in his belief that very young children cannot understand addition and subtraction: this assumption underlies most early mathematics schemes used in Britain today. For example, in their introduction to the Schools Council project *Early Mathematical Experiences* (1978), Geoffrey and Julia Matthews state that at the pre-school level 'There is so much to learn before even the simplest calculations have any meaning, that the idea of "sums for the very young child" is ludicrous.' Certainly there is a great deal of truth in that. Nevertheless, there is more to addition and subtraction than carrying out sums, and we should not passively accept the idea that young children understand little or nothing about the underlying processes involved.

The development of the Box task

My own interest in addition and subtraction arose almost by chance. One day I was playing some number games with a child called Gordon (4 years 8 months), from the Psychology Department Nursery at Edinburgh University. I produced a box containing bricks for him to count, but noticed that he was more interested in taking the bricks out of the box and putting them back in. It dawned on me that this situation was inherently attractive to him, and so I decided to develop it further.

Gordon had put ten bricks in the box. I asked him how many bricks were there. He counted them carefully, pointing to each brick in turn. 'There's ten,' he said. I took the box from him, removed three bricks in such a way that he could see the bricks taken out but could not see how many were left in the box, and shut the lid.

MH: I've taken three out. How many are left?
Gordon: I don't know. Five?
MH: Have a look and see. (Opens box.)
Gordon: (Counts bricks.) Seven!
MH: (Removes one brick and closes lid again.) I've taken another one out. How many are left now?
Gordon: I don't know. (Opens box and counts.) Six!

I decided to simplify the task, and emptied all the bricks out of the box. Gordon watched as I put two bricks back in and shut the lid.

MH: How many in the box now?
Gordon: Two.
MH: (Adds one brick in such a way that Gordon sees it going in but cannot see into the box.) How many now?
Gordon: Three.
MH: I'm putting one more in. (Adds one more, the same way.)
Gordon: Four. Four!
MH: And now I'm putting in two more. (Does so.)
Gordon: Six! Six!
MH: (Takes one brick out.) How many now?
Gordon: (Pause.) Five. Five!

MH: (Takes two out but does not have to ask the question.)
Gordon: Three!
MH: Do you want to see if you're right? (Opens the box.)
Gordon: (Throws arms open wide.) See!

Gordon was obviously intrigued by the problems I was setting him, and got quite excited when he thought he had the right answer. He evidently accepted as genuine the problem of working out what was in the box, and his replies suggested that he was capable of carrying out some simple additions and subtractions. Admittedly he had had some difficulty with the initial problems, but he easily managed the later ones when the numbers involved were smaller.

I decided to pursue the Box task further, and tried out various versions of it with twenty-three children from the Department Nursery. One of the main roles of the Nursery is to provide a supply of children for various projects based in the Department, and so the children were used to going out of the Nursery with an adult and playing games or solving problems in a one-to-one situation: because of this they were probably more sophisticated than the average pre-school child, and more relaxed and confident with a strange adult. The children were aged from 2 years 9 months to 4 years 11 months, and came from predominantly middle-class homes.

Each child was given a number of problems similar to that given to Gordon. Each problem had the same basic structure. First, the child identified how many bricks were in the box. Then bricks were added or taken away, so that the child could see – and was told – what had been done, but could not see the results of this action. Their problem was always to work out how many bricks were now in the box. Finally, they were allowed to look in the box and check their answer.

Most of the other children found the Box task as appealing and enjoyable as Gordon had done. They liked to shake the box to hear the bricks rattling around inside, and they also liked looking in the box after they had answered a question to see if they were right. Moreover, the task seemed to avoid the misinterpretations to which some of Piaget's tasks are open. With the Box task the children clearly see what the problem is. They know there are bricks in the box and can hear them if the box is shaken; at the same time, they cannot see the bricks, and so cannot say immediately how many there are. The problem is thus real and meaningful for the children in the way that some of Piaget's tasks are not: in Margaret Donaldson's terms 'it makes human sense'.

The meaningful nature of the task almost certainly enabled the children to show their capabilities. Provided the numbers involved were small (three bricks or fewer), even the youngest children (2 years 9 months to 3 years 2 months) could understand and succeed on the task. They could usually say how many bricks were in the box when it was open, and maintained that there was still the same number of bricks in the box after it had been closed. Most of them could also perform simple additions and subtractions, such as two bricks added to one brick, or one brick taken from two bricks. Interestingly enough, they had no greater difficulty with subtractions that resulted in zero: they clearly understood that one brick (or two bricks) taken from one brick (or two bricks) left nothing in the box.

There was quite a gap, however, between the children's ability to handle small numbers and their ability to handle slightly larger numbers. Only seven of the twenty-three children achieved even moderate success with numbers larger than three, and the youngest of these children was 4 years 5 months.

Some of these older children were very impressive in their performance. A good example is Richard (4 years 9 months). Richard responded correctly to the following problems: five bricks and one more, six bricks and two more, one brick taken from eight, two bricks taken from seven, and three bricks taken from five. This left two bricks in the box. I decided to press him with an apparently impossible subtraction:

MH: I want to take three bricks out of the box now.
Richard: You can't, can you?
MH: Why not?
Richard: You just have to put one in, don't you?
MH: Put one in?
Richard: Yeah, and then you can take three out.

Richard was clearly in full control of the situation and refused to be stumped by this impossible request. Moreover, his answer to the last question showed that he was capable of carrying out two successive mental calculations: the addition of one brick to two bricks, and the subsequent removal of all three bricks.

Children's strategies in the Box task

It is not surprising that the children should find small numbers easier to cope with than large numbers. Several research studies (such as Cowan, 1979; Gelman and Gallistel, 1978; Young and McPherson, 1976) have reported a similar phenomenon in other areas of number development, and indeed it makes a good deal of intuitive sense. Small numbers are clearly much easier to deal with than large numbers. The interesting question is whether we in fact deal with small numbers *in a different way* from large numbers. It has often been suggested, for example, that we can judge the number of items in a small visible group by a direct process of visual apprehension sometimes called 'subitising' (e.g. Klahr and Wallace, 1973). For numbers larger than four this process becomes less reliable, and we usually have to count instead.

The children's spoken comments as they worked on the problems suggested that they were in fact using different strategies for small-number and large-number versions of the Box task. For problems involving small numbers, they would either simply name the final quantity of bricks, or count up to that number as if they had constructed some sort of image or representation of the bricks in the box. Thus for one brick added to two bricks, the children would often count aloud 'One, two, three'. In contrast, most children who succeeded on large-number problems appeared to be using a different strategy based on *counting on* from the *initial* quantity. For example, if there were six bricks in the box and two more added, they would typically respond: 'Six, seven, eight, there's eight in the box.' For subtraction, they would have to work down the scale. This 'counting-on' procedure is quite complex, as children must keep track of how many steps they have moved up or down the scale. That is, they must in some way monitor their own thinking processes.

Further evidence of these two different strategies came from children who *used their fingers* to represent the contents of the box. Usually this only occurred with small-number problems, and involved the representation of the *final* number of bricks in the box. For example, Liam (2 years 11 months) was faced with the problem of one brick in the box and one more added. He held up two fingers and counted them, 'One, two.' When a third brick was added to the box, he held up three fingers, but miscounted: 'Three, four, nine, ten.' He seemed to have the basic idea but was let down by his limited ability to count. Juliette (3 years 0 months) was another child who used her fingers. For three bricks in the box she held up three fingers and counted, 'One, two, three.' For four bricks in the box she held up four fingers and counted, 'One, two, three, four, there's four in the box.' For five bricks she opened five fingers and said, 'One, two, three, four.' She then closed one finger and said, 'There's four.' She seemed to place more reliance on her faulty counting procedure than on her initial (and correct) representation of bricks with fingers.

Other children used an intriguing strategy which seemed to rely on a direct *visual image* of the bricks. These children tapped at different places on the closed lid of the box while answering, as if the lid was transparent and they were counting the bricks inside. As with the finger strategy, this was almost entirely restricted to small-number problems. One example was Angus (2 years 9 months), who was faced with one brick in the box and a second brick added. Angus tapped twice on the lid of the box, saying 'One, two' as he did so. Then he said, 'That one, that one,' again tapping twice on the lid. John (4 years 2 months) was given the same problem. He pointed to the lid twice and said, 'One, two.'

This strategy was less likely to be used when the numbers involved were five or more. In fact, there was only one example of a child tapping on the lid of the box when a large number was inside. This child was Kirsty (3 years 6 months) and there were five bricks in the box. She counted, 'One, two, three, four,' pointing each time to the lid of the box. It is possible that Kirsty was unsuccessful because she was unable to construct and retain in memory an image of more than four bricks.

Most of the children who used the counting-on strategy to solve large-number problems could also count the number of bricks correctly when they were in full view. An interesting exception to this was Andrew (4 years 9 months). Andrew knew his number sequence thoroughly from one to ten, but was consistently poor at counting rows of bricks. In the following session he is successful three times at adding on when the box is closed, but on two other occasions he is unable to count the bricks accurately when the box is open. In the first sequence three bricks were in the box, and two have been added:

MH: How many in the box?
Andrew: Five.
MH: (Opens box.) Shall we have a look?
Andrew: (Miscounts.) One, two, three, four.

Later, six bricks were in the box, and one had been added:

MH: How many now?
Andrew: Seven.
MH: (Adds two more) How many now?
Andrew: Eight. Nine.
MH: Eight or nine?
Andrew: Nine.
MH: (Opens box.) Count them and see.
Andrew: (Miscounts.) One, two, three, four, five, six, seven, eight.

Addition and subtraction: a further study

These children in the Department Nursery seemed able to carry out a surprisingly wide range of simple additions and subtractions. They could not, however, be regarded as a representative sample of pre-school children. Accordingly I carried out a further study involving a total of sixty children (twenty-eight boys and thirty-two girls) aged 3 to 5 years. The children came from two distinct and contrasting areas of Edinburgh. Half the children attended school in a comfortable middle-class area: their fathers were almost exclusively in professional or managerial occupations, such as architects or accountants. The other thirty children attended school in a severely deprived working-class part of the city, where social problems were profound: in this area, the children's fathers were in manual occupations, unemployed or (quite frequently) absent. Within each school ten children were chosen at random from each of the 3-year-old, 4-year-old and 5-year-old age groups. The youngest group had just started nursery class, the middle group had been attending nursery class for a year and the oldest group had just started in the reception class in the primary school. None of the children had received any formal instruction in addition or subtraction, and only three out of the sixty succeeded on a standard Piagetian number-conservation task. (For more details of this study, see Hughes, 1981.)

Overall, the performance of this sample of children was very similar to that of the Department Nursery children. Almost all the children were successful on small-number versions of the Box task, with their performance being particularly high (just under 90 per cent) on problems involving the addition or subtraction of a single brick (one brick added to one brick, one brick taken from two bricks, and one brick taken from one brick). Problems involving the addition or subtraction of two bricks were slightly harder, but still about 75 per cent of the children were able to work out the result of adding two bricks to one brick, or taking two bricks from three bricks. As before, additions and subtractions involving a larger initial group (five bricks or more) were considerably harder, but even these were completed successfully by over a quarter of the children.

This larger study also gave further support to the idea that the children use different strategies for the small-number and large-number problems. As before, some children used their fingers to represent the overall number of bricks for small-number problems, while others explicitly used the counting-on strategy for large-number problems. There was also some indirect evidence for these different strategies in the relative success rate for addition and subtraction problems. If the children were performing the small-number problems by constructing some representation of the final amount, and then counting this final amount, then we would not expect any difference in the relative difficulty of problems involving addition and those involving subtraction. This indeed was what I found for the small-number problems: children were just as successful on addition problems as on subtraction problems. However, a different pattern might be expected for the large-number problems. If children's strategy on these problems is to count up or down the number scale, starting from the initial contents of the box, then one might expect that addition would be easier than subtraction. After all, children have more experience counting up the number scale (five, six, seven) than counting down (seven, six, five). Again, this was confirmed: I found that, for the large-number problems, children were more successful with addition than with subtraction.

I also used this study to find out how children would perform on addition and subtraction problems that were different in various ways from the Box task. I wanted to know how children would respond if they were asked *hypothetical* questions such as, 'If there was one brick in the box and I added two more, how many would there be?' or 'If there was one child in a shop and two more went in, how many children would be in the shop now?' I wanted to see if these problems, which involved specific but hypothetical objects, were any harder than the immediately visible Box task. I also wanted to know how children would respond when given the same problems but expressed in the more formal language of arithmetic: 'What does one and two make?' or 'What does two take away one make?'

TABLE 3.1   Overall performance on addition/subtraction problems (%)

	Box closed	Hypothetical box	Hypothetical shop	Formal code
Small numbers	83	56	62	15
Large numbers	28	20	23	6

Let us look at performance on the two hypothetical problems first. As table 3.1 shows, over half the children were successful on small-number versions of these two problems, and nearly a quarter were successful on large-number versions. Clearly these problems are not totally beyond the grasp of pre-school children. Indeed, the children's performance on these hypothetical problems appears at first sight to resemble their performance on the Box task. Closer inspection, however, revealed a statistically significant difference between the hypothetical problems and the Box task but for *small numbers only*. There was no such difference when the numbers were slightly larger.

Why should hypothetical problems be harder for small numbers only? One possibility is that this difference is related to the different strategies proposed earlier for small-number and large-number versions of the Box task. If children do construct some sort of image or representation for small-number problems, then this may well be helped by having the bricks and box actually present in front of them. If on the other hand they use the counting-on strategy for the large-number problems, then it would seem that the physical presence of the bricks gives only a minimal advantage.

What happened when the problems were phrased in the more formal language of arithmetic ('What does one and two make?')? As table 3.1 shows, only 15 per cent of the children were successful on small-number versions of these questions, and almost all of these correct responses were to the question 'What does one and one make?' Only two children were able to deal with formal problems involving slightly larger numbers (such as 'What does five and one make?'). These important findings will be discussed further in chapter 4.

Social-class differences

It is clear that pre-school children can carry out simple additions and subtractions, particularly when the numbers involved are small. However, these abilities are not uniformly distributed amongst all children. As figure 3.1 shows, there was a substantial difference between the middle-class and working-class children in their overall performance (that is, their total number of correct answers for all tasks combined, expressed as a percentage). This difference was equivalent to about a year's difference in age: the working-class 4-year-olds were performing at about the same level as the middle-class 3-year-olds, while the working-class 5-year-olds were performing at the same level as the middle-class 4-year-olds. As figure 3.1 shows, this gap is much the same size throughout the age-range.

It is not in itself surprising that there should be social-class differences in children's mathematical abilities. Such differences have been reported several times before – for example, in the large-scale National Child Development Study *From Birth to Seven* (Davie, Butler and Goldstein, 1972). What is striking here is the sheer size of the gap: a year's difference

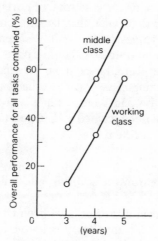

Figure 3:1 Age and social-class effects on overall performance on addition/ subtraction tasks

at age 4 years represents a considerable deficit, which will not easily be made up. It should be borne in mind that the social backgrounds of the children differed very sharply: the working-class children lived in an extremely deprived area, and the middle-class children in a very comfortable one. Nevertheless, it is disturbing to think that there should be so large a disparity between children's abilities at such an early stage in their lives.

It is also disturbing to note that there is no sign that attending nursery school is having any compensatory effect on the working-class children – the gap is just as large at the end of the pre-school period as at the beginning – although it is of course possible that the gap might otherwise have become even wider.

What might be the cause of this social-class difference? The most common explanation given for differences of this kind is that they reflect differences in the stimulation offered to young children in their homes. It has been argued that middle-class parents talk more to their children, and encourage them in intellectual pursuits, while working-class parents offer much less linguistic stimulation to their children. The evidence for this is in fact quite limited. Our detailed study of 4-year-olds in London found very few differences in the amount or kind of talk used by middle-class and by working-class mothers when conversing with their 4-year-old daughters (see Tizard and Hughes, 1984). However, while the children we studied in London were in two distinct social-class groupings, they may not have represented such extremes as the two groups of children studied in Edinburgh.

Whatever the explanation, it is always important to focus as much on what children *can* do as on what they lack in comparison with others. While the working-class 5-year-olds certainly lacked some of the abilities of their more fortunate middle-class counterparts, they still possessed important abilities – they were, for example, starting to use the counting-on strategy. All the working-class 3-year-olds had some notion of number – even the little girl who had seemed unable to count two bricks on her first interview exclaimed excitedly 'I'm coming two times!' as she came out on a second occasion.

Recent American research on addition and subtraction

In the last few years several studies have been carried out with young American children which essentially confirm the findings reported here. One study, by Prentice Starkey and Rochel Gelman (1982), used a task very similar to the Box task, in which children were asked to work out how many pennies were in an adult's hand. As in the Box task, the adult added or subtracted pennies in such a way that the child knew how many were being added or removed but was unable to see how many were left at the end. Starkey and Gelman reported that most children aged 3 to 5 years could carry out simple additions and subtractions in this manner. As in the Edinburgh study, problems involving small numbers were much easier than those involving slightly larger numbers. Moreover, the children in the American study appeared to use very similar strategies to those of the Edinburgh study. As Starkey and Gelman report (p. 102): 'Some children used fingers to represent the screened object; others counted aloud, apparently either imagining objects, or working directly off the sequence of number names.'

Further work by Starkey (1983) suggests that children even younger than these may understand simple additions and subtractions. In this study, twelve children aged from 24 to 35 months were first asked to put two, three or four objects one at a time into a container. After the child had done this, the experimenter would add another object to those in the container, or take one out, or leave the number unchanged. Next, the child was asked to remove all the objects one by one from the container. The container was constructed in such a way that the child could take out only one object at a time. It was thus assumed that each time the child reached into the container he or she was under the impression that at least one object was there. This task is again very similar to the Box task, but it does not require the child to understand the number words, 'one', 'two' and 'three'. Starkey reports that all but two of the children executed a 'numerically correct search' on most of the problems that involved numbers less than four. In contrast, only two children were successful when there were more than four objects in the container. According to Starkey, addition and subtraction problems were solved equally often. The results suggest that a capacity for simple addition and subtraction may be present in children even younger than the ones studied in the Edinburgh project.

Several recent American studies have reported not only that young children can carry out simple additions and subtractions, but that to do so they use strategies based on counting. In particular, it has been noted that children frequently progress from a 'counting-all' strategy (counting the final number of objects) to one based on counting on from the initial quantity (see Fuson, 1982). It has been pointed out several times that the counting-on strategy is not usually one that children have been taught. The inference is therefore that they have invented it for themselves.

There is a particularly interesting study by Guy Groen and Lauren Resnick (1977) which appears to demonstrate children inventing the counting-on strategy. This study was based on a technique by which children are given addition and subtraction problems, and the amount of time required to solve the problems is carefully noted; these reaction times are then used to determine the kind of strategy that the children use. In Groen and Resnick's study, a group of children aged around 5 years were taught to solve simple addition problems which were presented in written form. For example, the children were taught to respond to '2 + 3 =   ' by counting out two blocks, then counting out three more blocks, and then counting the combined set. After a number of practice sessions, the children were given various addition problems to solve without recourse to the blocks, and their answers were timed. This project continued over several weeks, and it was possible to notice whether or not the children's strategies changed. Groen and Resnick report that half the children made a clear switch from mentally counting all the objects to counting on from the larger number (i.e. they would count 'Three, four, five'). According to Groen and Resnick, this study demonstrates that young children can invent efficient strategies despite being taught alternative methods for solving the problem.

Overview

Recent research in Britain and the United States shows that children start school with considerable abilities in the area of simple addition and subtraction, provided that the numbers involved are small. These abilities are most likely to be elicited by clear concrete problems, the meaning of which children can easily grasp. A particularly suitable problem is one in which the additions or subtractions are carried out on real objects which the child can see, but where the final total is hidden in some way. This context may well represent a very fundamental human situation in which an addition or subtraction has to be calculated.

Such findings present a direct challenge to Piaget's theory. To be fair, Piaget himself admitted that pre-operational children may have some understanding of small numbers, but he dismissed this ability as 'intuitive' and gave little idea of how it fitted into his wider theory. He was, moreover, repeatedly critical of young children's use of counting, suggesting that this was a skill in which children could be trained by parents, but of which they had little understanding. The work described in this chapter suggests the opposite: children's counting strategies are frequently untaught, and are meaningful attempts by the children to solve the problems confronting them.

These findings also present problems for understanding what happens to children in school. If we had found that children possessed very few abilities on starting school, then perhaps their subsequent difficulty with school mathematics might be easier to accept. Instead, we have something of a paradox: young children appear to start school with more mathematical knowledge than has hitherto been thought. In that case, why should they experience such difficulty with school mathematics?

4

What's so hard
about two and two?

By the time they start school at around 5 years, most children can carry
out a range of simple additions and subtractions involving both concrete
and hypothetical situations. They know that two bricks added to one
already in a box results in three bricks in the box, and that if there is
one child in a shop and two more go in then there will be three children
in the shop. However, when asked 'What does two and one make?',
very few children can answer correctly.

At first sight, this disparity does not seem too surprising. We feel
intuitively that questions like 'What does two and one make?' will be
harder for young children than questions about bricks in boxes, or about
children in a shop. But in what does this hardness consist? As we will
see in this chapter, the answer to this question is not as straightforward
as it might seem.

Locating the source of children's difficulties

One possibility that I had to consider was that the children's difficulties
were caused by the presence of the words 'make' and 'take away' in
such questions as 'What does one and two make?' and 'What does two
take away one make?' Young children frequently have difficulties when
familiar words such as these are used in an unfamiliar context: they may
well associate 'make' with constructive activities like playing with Lego,
while 'take away' might be associated more with Chinese food than with
number.

If this were the only cause of children's difficulties, then they would
be more successful when asked questions like 'How many is two and
one?', 'How many is two and one more?', 'How many is one taken from

three?' and so on. However, when I tried these alternative wordings with children from the Psychology Department Nursery I found that they made no difference to the children's performance. It seemed that children's difficulties arose whenever phrases such as 'two and one' *did not refer to any specific objects.*

At about this time I came across an even more direct demonstration of this point. In the large-scale study of addition and subtraction described in the last chapter, the children had been presented with a series of problems within a particular category. For example, when given Hypothetical Shop problems, they would be asked a series of questions about children going into a shop. When I played through videotapes which I had made of these sessions, I noticed that something interesting was happening. In the course of repeating a series of questions on the same topic, I occasionally omitted to mention the topic in question. For example, towards the end of a series of Hypothetical Shop questions, I might phrase a question in the following way: 'Five and one more, how many is that?' What was interesting was that *in this situation* the children appeared not to notice that the words 'children' and 'shop' had been omitted. It seemed that, once they were 'locked into' a series of questions on a particular topic, they did not need the topic spelled out to them every time.

My omission of the topic in the Hypothetical Shop questions had been purely accidental. Having noticed this omission, however, I deliberately made the same error with a further small group of children. The conversation below with Adrian (4 years 1 month) is a typical result of this policy. Adrian had been doing the Box task with a real box and bricks, and we had arrived at a situation where there were ten bricks in the box.

MH: Let's just put one more in. (Does so.) Ten and one more, how many is that?
Adrian: Er...(Thinks.)...Eleven!
MH: Yes, very good. Let's just put one more in. (Does so.) Eleven and one more, how many is that?
Adrian: Twelve!

Five minutes later the following sequence of questions took place. This time the bricks had been put away and there were no materials on the table.

MH: I'm going to ask you some questions. Okay? How many is two and one more? (No response.) Two and one more, how many is that?
Adrian: Er...makes...

MH: Makes – how many?
Adrian: Er...fifteen (in a couldn't-care-less tone of voice).

Notice that exactly the same wording appears in each dialogue. The difference is that in the first dialogue the question 'Ten and one more, how many is that?' refers to bricks, and here Adrian shows considerable skill; in the second dialogue the question 'Two and one more, how many is that?' does not obviously refer to anything, and now Adrian does not seem able to add even one and two.

It has been suggested more than once that my interpretation of the dialogues is incorrect, and that Adrian's final response, 'Fifteen', in the second conversation is, in fact, a sign of remarkable skill on his part. This alternative explanation claims that Adrian is starting where he finished off the previous conversation, with a set of twelve bricks, and that he adds on 'two and one more' to reach fifteen. If Adrian was in fact doing this it would be an even more startling demonstration of children's abilities to perform additions with the Box task. All the same, this alternative explanation seems to me unlikely. Five minutes had passed between the conversations, during which Adrian had made a train with the bricks, put them away in the box, and told me in some detail about the 'Goldilocks and the Three Bears' story that he had been hearing in the nursery. In addition, his final answer of 'Fifteen' was said in a couldn't-care-less tone of voice, which contrasted strongly with the excited way in which he had answered 'Eleven' and 'Twelve' in the first conversation. Although he was asked some further questions along the lines of 'Two and one more, how many is that?', he was unable to answer any of them.

A question of abstraction?

It appears, then that most children start school at 5 years able to carry out simple additions and subtractions, provided these take place in contexts involving specific objects, people or events. In contrast, when they are presented with similar additions and subtractions in contexts where there is no reference to specific objects, they are usually unable to answer. How are we to explain this phenomenon?

One possible approach lies in the idea of *abstraction*. It might be argued that children will only understand 'Two and two makes four' when they have abstracted what is common from a large number of specific examples – such as two bricks and two bricks making four bricks, two houses and two houses making four houses and so on. From this point of view pre-school children have a certain degree of concrete understanding, but have not yet performed the necessary abstraction.

This position bears some resemblance to Piaget's theory, in that it emphasises that concepts are formed through interaction with the physical environment. However, Piaget himself did not use the term 'abstraction', and in any case regarded the acquisition of mathematical concepts as a spin-off from more general intellectual development. Much greater emphasis on abstraction is given by Richard Skemp, in his influential book *The Psychology of Learning Mathematics* (1971). According to Skemp (p. 161), mathematical concepts are, as a rule, built up by the process of abstraction from concrete examples.

> Just as 5 represents the property common to all sets which match the standard set ('one', 'two', 'three', 'four', 'five'), so $5 + 7 = 12$ represents what is common to all acts of uniting sets like the above, whatever may be the particular sets involved. . . . As beginners, we learn that any five-set united with any seven-set make a twelve-set. Abstracting, we say 'five and seven make twelve', or $5 + 7 = 12$ . . . . It is by working with sets of physical objects that we first develop these and similar concepts.

The idea of abstraction has a certain amount of appeal. There is no doubt that statements like 'Two and two makes four' are more abstract than statements about bricks. Moreover, such statements do indeed encapsulate some property common to a large number of concrete examples. However, the more I pondered the explanation that children arrive at 'Two and two makes four' simply through a process of 'abstraction', the more I felt dissatisfied with it.

To start with, I was unhappy with the implications of the 'abstraction' account for what we actually do to help young children. The theory seems to suggest that, when faced with children apparently lacking an abstract concept, we must present them with further concrete experiences and hope that the process of 'abstracting' will take place spontaneously. It seemed to me that the children I had studied already had sufficient understanding at the concrete level of what happened when two small groups of objects were combined. Their difficulty lay rather in *going beyond these concrete experiences*, and merely to provide more such experiences did not seem particularly relevant.

Indeed, it seemed on further reflection that those children who had successfully answered some Hypothetical Shop questions already had a concept of addition and subtraction that was to some degree abstract: they must have abstracted in order to apply their understanding of addition and subtraction to these relatively unfamiliar problems. True, they certainly knew what it meant to go into a shop, but nevertheless the specific calculations involved were ones they were unlikely to have come across before. Interestingly enough, I obtained some support for this view from an earlier statement in Richard Skemp's book (p. 27) that:

> The criterion for having a concept is not that of being able to say its name, but that of *behaving in a way indicative of classifying new data according to the similarities which go to form this concept.* (my italics)

Was it possible then that these Edinburgh children had indeed already abstracted the relevant concepts, but did not know how to express them? This implied the possibility – ignored by the 'abstraction' account – that children's difficulties may to a large extent be caused by the language with which they must express their abstraction. In other words, their difficulties may have been in understanding and using the particular form of language in statements like 'Two and two makes four.'

This point may become clearer by considering an analogy. Suppose we ask young children questions like 'What does yellow and blue make?', and find that they cannot reply (this question is analogous to 'What does two and one make?')? We might conclude that they lack an adequate concept of colour-mixing, or even that they have no colour concepts at all. We might also conclude that they therefore need further specific experiences of colour-mixing in order to develop this knowledge.

What, however, if we were to find that at the same time they had little difficulty in answering questions like 'If you mixed yellow paint with blue paint, what colour would you get?' (questions analogous to the Hypothetical Box or Shop questions)? In that case, we would surely have to revise our conclusion. The children do, after all, understand the process of colour-mixing. Their difficulties would seem to be specifically caused by the question 'What does yellow and blue make?' We would have to conclude that their limitations lie in not understanding the meaning of these questions, rather than with the underlying concepts, and we would probably attempt to remedy the situation by explaining what these questions mean, and how they relate to specific exemplars.

Like all analogies this one should not be pressed too far. Colour words, as we shall see, differ in various interesting ways from number words. Nevertheless, the analogy suggests that we should pay much more attention to the language of mathematics – even that we should consider mathematics as a language in itself.

Mathematics as a language

The last few years have seen an increasing acceptance of the idea that we need to consider mathematics as a language. Indeed, to the surprise of many of its readers, this was given central importance by the Cockroft report in 1982. The first chapter of the report attempts to answer the question of why we should teach mathematics at all. It points out that mathematics has many uses – as the basis of science and technology, as satisfying the arithmetical requirements of home and work, and even as a management tool in commerce or industry. However, the report goes on (para. 3):

> *We believe that all these perceptions of the usefulness of mathematics arise from the fact that mathematics provides a means of communication which is powerful, concise and unambiguous.* Even though many of those who consider mathematics to be useful would probably not express the reason in these terms, we believe that it is the fact that mathematics can be used as a powerful means of communication which provides the principal reason for teaching mathematics to all children. (emphasis in the original)

Certainly the idea that mathematics is a kind of language fits in very well with the intuitive feelings of many learners of mathematics. Unfortunately, for many of these learners mathematics does not feel like a language with which they are at home, but more like an unfamiliar foreign language. The clearest statement I have encountered of this feeling comes from the 'Peanuts' cartoon reproduced in figure 4.1.

The same sentiment has been expressed about the comprehension of mathematics, as well as its production:

> Mathematicians are a sort of Frenchman. Whenever you say anything to them, they translate it into their own language and right away it is something completely different. (Goethe, quoted in Pimm, 1983).

Clearly, there are many ways in which learning mathematics does not resemble learning a foreign language. One difference which we have already encountered is that the language of mathematics contains many familiar English words. Words and phrases such as 'makes', 'take away', 'difference', 'times', 'borrow', 'carry' and 'goes into', are all part of the vocabulary of arithmetic, where their uses are slightly and subtly different from their uses in ordinary conversation. This can often be the cause of unexpected difficulty for children. I can recall very well the day when Sally, my 7-year-old stepdaughter, came home from school and showed me her two attempts to answer the subtraction problem 'What is the difference between 11 and 6?' Her first answer had been '11 has two numbers', but this had been marked wrong. Her second attempt was '6 is curly', but this had also been treated as incorrect.

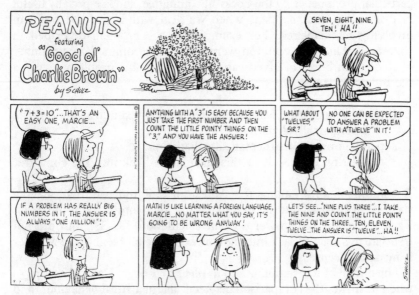

Figure 4.1 'Maths is like learning a foreign language, Marcie...'
(© 1980 United Features Syndicate, Inc.)

One crucial task for the learner of mathematics is therefore to recognise when 'mathematics is being spoken' (see Pimm, 1983). This aspect of learning mathematics has received little attention to date, and we do not know when and how children come to acquire this 'meta-linguistic' skill. The following dialogue with Alison (4 years 7 months) shows that some children may in fact be capable of recognising some aspects of the language of mathematics at a very early age.

MH: What does one and two make?
Alison: I can't answer questions like that.
MH: Why not?
Alison: Because I don't go to school yet.

This response suggests a perceptive identification of the kind of language being used, and an accurate location of the context where it is most frequently found.

If we pursue the linguistic analogy further, then it makes sense to suggest that children have to learn to *translate* between the language of mathematics and their ordinary knowledge about familiar things and situations. As we saw in chapter 1, this idea of translation was given particular prominence by the Cockroft committee, and is especially useful in describing what happens when we deal with a real-life problem involving mathematics. For example, in the problem described in chapter 1, American children were asked to accommodate a number of soldiers in buses of given capacity. Solving this problem required the following steps:

1 translating the problem from its real-life context into an appropriate mathematical calculation;
2 performing the mathematical calculation;
3 translating the result of this calculation back into the context.

A common failing among the American children was that, having successfully carried out the first two steps, they forgot about the third. They arrived at the answer to their calculation, '31.33', but did not translate this answer back into the context of the problem to see whether it made any sense.

The notion of translation is also implied by Robert Davis (1984, p. 4) when he makes the comparison between 'mathematical behaviour' and singing in a foreign language: both can occur as a successful imitation or as founded on understanding. The kind of mathematical behaviour which consists merely in correct responses to certain cues would presumably satisfy a behaviourist such as Thorndike (see chapter 2), but the parallel suggested by Davis is an illuminating one: as we shall see later on, it is often very useful to think about children's mathematical understanding in terms of their ability – or inability – to carry out particular translations.

Linking the abstract and the concrete

It may be helpful to summarise the argument so far. Children aged around 4 to 5 years have a good understanding of simple additions and subtractions involving specific objects or events. However, they are unable to answer questions such as 'What does one and two make?'

While it is possible to see this as simply showing that they have failed to 'abstract', there are limitations to this point of view. Instead, it may be more fruitful to consider questions like 'What does one and two make?' as children's first encounters with a new form of language – the language of mathematics.

The most immediate linguistic problem caused by such questions, as we have already seen, is that they do not refer to any specific objects or events. This of course is what makes arithmetic such a powerful tool for thinking and problem-solving: it can be applied to a variety of different contexts. However, it is precisely this abstract or context-free nature of arithmetic statements that is the source of much of children's difficulty with them. In the following conversation, Ram (4 years 7 months) makes his puzzlement quite explicit:

MH: What is three and one more? How many is three and one more?
Ram: Three and what? One what? Letter? I mean number? [We had earlier been playing a game with magnetic numerals and Ram is presumably referring to them here.]
MH: How many is three and one more?
Ram: One more what?
MH: Just one more, you know?
Ram: (Disgruntled) I *don't* know.

A fundamental strategy in comprehending spoken language is to locate the topic, to ask: 'What is this utterance about?' As Ram's response makes clear, questions like 'What is three and one more?' are thus employing language in a way radically different from the way in which children are accustomed to hearing language used and for which they have developed appropriate skills.

Ram's response, which shows his attempt to locate the topic of my question, is unusual in that he is explicitly prepared to translate the abstract question into concrete form. In fact, when pre-school children are asked questions like 'What does two and one make?', they usually reply with a number which has no apparent relevance to the problem. Very few children appear to reason along the following lines: 'Well I don't know what one and two makes, but I do know that one brick and two bricks makes three bricks, so maybe the answer is three.' Naturally, one would not expect pre-school children to verbalise the problem in exactly this way, but their thinking might well proceed along such lines.

It might be thought that this is an unlikely thing for young children to do. However, the findings of a study I carried out some years ago with Robert Grieve would certainly encourage such an expectation (Hughes and Grieve, 1980). In this study we asked children aged 5 years and 7 years questions which were in some sense bizarre. For example, the children were asked, 'Is red bigger than yellow?' To our surprise, we found that virtually all the children treated these questions seriously and constructed sensible meanings for them. A specific strategy which several of the children used was to translate the questions into a meaningful context. One child, for instance, looked round the room and then replied that yellow was bigger than red, explaining that 'That red cushion there is smaller than that yellow curtain there'.

If children spontaneously translate unusual questions involving colour into a specific context, then it is reasonable to suppose that they might be encouraged to do the same with 'unusual' questions involving number. In an attempt to facilitate this process, I used a procedure in which a small group of pre-school children were presented with questions phrased in the abstract language of arithmetic interposed with questions about particular objects. Even with this procedure, though, the children showed a surprising reluctance to translate between the two kinds of question. The following dialogue with Amanda (3 years 11 months) is typical:

MH: How many is two and one? (Long pause. No response.) Well how many bricks is two bricks and one brick?
Amanda: Three.
MH: Okay. So how many is two and one?
Amanda: (Pause.) Four (hesitantly)?
MH: How many is one brick and one more brick?
Amanda: Two bricks.
MH: So how many is one and one?
Amanda: One, maybe.

Amanda clearly saw no connection between the questions concerned with bricks and the more abstract questions – indeed, she seems to be using a strategy of giving a *different* response to the latter. It is as if she is thinking, 'Well I don't understand this question, but I know it's not the same as the previous one, so I'll try a different answer.'

This conversation with Amanda shows that juxtaposing questions in the language of arithmetic with those referring to concrete situations does not necessarily ensure that children will see a connection between the two. All the same, this is a tactic which teachers often use in the classroom. In her article 'Discussion and the Teaching of Mathematics' (1983), Hilary Shuard analyses a conversation in which a boy called Jeremy (aged about 8) had difficulty with a multiplication problem. In this problem he was told that Mary had three times as many bricks as John, and that John had eight bricks. The task was to work out how many bricks Mary had.

[The teacher is speaking.]
If Mary's got three times as many . . .
How many bricks has Mary got then?
(Pause)
Mary's got three times as many bricks as John.
John's got eight bricks.
She's got three times as many.

This line of questioning was not getting any response, so the teacher tried a different one.

What's three times eight then?
(Pause)
J: *Twenty-three?*
(Teacher silently indicates disagreement)
(Pause)
J: *Twenty-four?*

Jeremy then went on to a further question in which Andrew had four times as many bricks as John. In the course of discussing this further question, it emerged that Jeremy thought he should carry out an addition rather than a multiplication. Shuard points out (p. 22) that 'To Jeremy, "3 times 8" may have seemed to be an irrelevant and islolated question, independent of the problem about Mary's bricks. . . . Even if he satisfactorily completed the set of problems by multiplying, we do not know whether he knew *why* multiplication was the correct operation to use.'

A similar point can be made about the following conversation with Patrick (4 years 1 month), in which I adopted a slightly different approach. I presented Patrick with a series of questions about a variety of specific objects, followed by the corresponding abstract question. I thought it possible that this approach might emphasise what was common to the series and facilitate any process of 'making sense' that might have been available.

MH: How many is two and one more?
Patrick: Four.
MH: Well, how many is two *lollipops* and one more?
Patrick: Three.

MH: How many is two *elephants* and one more?
Patrick: Three.
MH: How many is two *giraffes* and one more?
Patrick: Three.
MH: So how many is *two* and one more?
Patrick: Six.

This approach was on the surface no more successful than either of the previous conversations quoted above. There was, however, a noticeable suggestion of defiance in the way Patrick looked me straight in the eye as he gave his final answer 'Six.' Perhaps he did after all know, from the way the question had been introduced, that he was expected to say 'Three' but, for a reason which we shall never know, he was refusing to do so.

It is puzzling that children find questions involving colour words easier to translate into specific contexts than those involving number words. This may reflect some particular property of our own number words, such as 'one' and 'two'. There are some cultures, for example, where the connection between the number words and the numbers being represented is made more directly. Karl Menninger (1969) describes an early Indian system in which the word for 'one' is the same as the word for 'moon', the word for 'two' the same as that for 'eyes', that for 'four' the same as that for 'brother' (in Indian mythology Rama was one of four brothers), the word for 'seven' the same as that for 'head' (the head has seven openings), and so on. Other systems use the words for 'hand' to mean 'five', 'two hands' to mean 'ten', and 'a whole man' to mean 'twenty' (see p. 82). It is possible that young children would find it easier to learn arithmetic if our own number system contained similar links between number words and concrete objects.

Using fingers to link the abstract and the concrete

My attempts to introduce the abstract language of arithmetic to pre-school children had led to some interesting failures. I wondered whether parents of pre-school children did this kind of thing at home and, if so, how they did it. I was able to answer this question by looking at a large number of conversations between young children and their mothers which we had collected in a previous study (Tizard and Hughes, 1984). The children were aged from 3 years 9 months to 4 years 3 months, and were recorded during their everyday interactions at home.

There were in fact relatively few conversations in our transcripts where the children's mothers were explicitly using the language of arithmetic. However, those which did occur revealed some interesting features.

The following conversation between Susan and her mother arose when they were singing the traditional children's song about currant buns in the baker's shop. This song describes a progressive reduction in the number of buns in the shop as they are sold. The usual practice is to start with five and work down until there are no buns left. Susan's mother at one point stopped singing to explain:

Mother: If you've got three current buns in the baker's shop, look! (holds up three fingers) – and I take one away (folds one finger down), how many are left?
Susan: (Doesn't answer, but carries on singing) Three currant buns in the baker's shop...
Mother: How many are left if I take one away from three? (She holds up three fingers again and folds one down.)
Susan: Two.
Mother: That's right.
Susan: Three (starts to sing)...
Mother: No, *two* currant buns in the shop.
Susan: Two currant buns in the baker's shop...Round and flat with sugar on top...Come a boy with a penny one day...(Stops.) Put your hand up with two fingers. (Mother does so.) Along come a boy with a penny one day...(Susan folds one finger down.)
Mother: How many's left now?
Susan: (Sings.) One currant bun in the baker – (Stops singing.) Put your finger out! (Mother holds up one finger and Susan continues singing) Along come a boy – and took it away. (Stops singing.) None left.
Mother: None left now!

What is interesting here is the way Susan's mother uses her fingers to stand for the buns (in some nursery classes this is done by actually using the children themselves to represent the buns). Thus the question 'How many are left if I take one away from three?', which originally referred to imaginary buns, now refers to the immediately present fingers. The value of this aid is clear from Susan's demand that it be used again later in the song.

A similar strategy was used by Donna's mother in the following conversation, in relation to the number of cakes that would be needed for tea. Donna, however, had a less secure grasp of basic counting skills than Susan:

Mother: Well if you're gonna have two and Daddy's gonna have two (first holds up two fingers, then another two) – how many's that?

Donna: Three.
Mother: No.
Donna: Four.
Mother: That's right! And if Mummy's gonna have another two, what's that? Four, and two? (Holds up two more fingers.)
Donna: Four and...
Mother: If that's four, that one makes? (She holds up four fingers and then one more.)
Donna: Five.
Mother: And that one makes? (Adds another finger.)
Donna: Four.
Mother: No, these are five (Points to the five already up).
Donna: Five.
Mother: Five and one more is?
Donna: Six.
Mother: That's right! Now if you're gonna have two, Mummy's gonna have two and Daddy's gonna have two, that's six, and if Kerry's gonna have two that's, that's six (holds up six fingers) and one more makes?
Donna: Five.
Mother: No.
Donna: Six.
Mother: Yeah, and what's after six?
Donna: Eight?
Mother: No.

In both these conversations, the abstract language of arithmetic is used in conjunction with fingers to solve a problem involving specific but absent objects. A further example of this kind of problem-solving occurred when another child, Jane, was playing in the garden with her friends. She returned to the kitchen and asked for some glasses of orange juice to take out as a picnic. Her mother wanted to know how many children were there altogether, and suggested that Jane held up a finger for each child in the garden. They finally worked out by this method how many glasses of orange juice were required.

We described several children in chapter 3 using their fingers in a similar way to represent bricks which they knew were in the box but which they could not see. These conversations suggest that the use of fingers to represent unseen objects is a tactic which they may have observed their parents using at home. This is not to suggest that parents are consciously 'drilling' children in this particular strategy. Rather it seems that using fingers is a natural and obvious way of representing groups of objects. Fingers have the tremendous advantage that they are always with us, and that they are easy to manipulate: we can put up fingers, keep them there for as long as we want to inspect and count them, and bend them down to represent objects being taken away.

It is a small but crucial step from the use of fingers to represent absent objects to the use of fingers to explore relationships between numbers. The following conversation occurred when Mary was sitting at dinner with her mother. Apparently out of the blue, she held up two fingers of each hand and asked:

Mary: Does two and two make four?
Mother: Mmm.
Mary: Three and three makes...(Holds up three fingers on each hand and counts them.) One, two, three, four, five, six.
Mother: Mmm.
Mary: Count this! (Holds up four fingers on each hand and counts.) One, two, three, four, five, six, seven, eight.
Mother: Well done! Yes, that's right.

Here, Mary is not using her fingers to solve a specific problem but is instead using them to give a concrete referent to her use of the language of arithmetic. We do not know what experiences led up to this conversation, but it seems highly likely that using fingers in the way seen with Susan, Donna and Jane would lead on to this more abstract usage.

Fingers can thus play a crucial role in linking the abstract and the concrete, because they can be both representations of objects and objects in their own right. As we shall see in the next chapter, this property is also shared with another fundamental device: the use of a written mark or tally to represent an object.

Overview

In this chapter I have argued that children's difficulties with questions such as 'What does one and two make?' can usefully be seen as stemming from their failure to understand a new kind of language, the language of mathematics. There are many aspects to this language, such as its unfamiliarity and its lack of concrete referents, which cause children difficulty. While they may have an abstract understanding of number in the sense that they can apply their knowledge to new situations, they cannot express this knowledge in the abstract and formal language of mathematics. Children need to develop links – *or ways of translating* – between this new language and their own concrete knowledge. These translations are of fundamental importance in understanding mathematics.

The ability to carry out such translations does not come easily to young children. One way they can be helped is with the familiar and fundamental device of using fingers. Fingers can be used both to represent absent objects (such as buns or children) and to stand in their own right as concrete referents for statements in the language of arithmetic. As such, they provide an important link between the abstract and the concrete.

5

Children's invention of written arithmetic

In the last chapter we saw how difficult young children find it to link their concrete understanding of number to statements expressed in the abstract language of arithmetic, such as 'One and two makes three', or 'Three take away two leaves one'. But the same statements can also be expressed in writing as '1 + 2 = 3', or '3 − 2 = 1'. It seems likely that children will find it even harder to connect their understanding with this formal written symbolism. Statements like '1 + 2 = 3' are not only abstract rather than concrete: they are also written rather than spoken, and use the relatively unfamiliar symbols of arithmetic.

Although they see written numerals around them all the time, children in most Western societies are not usually introduced to written arithmetic until they start school. The exact age at which this takes place varies from country to country but, whenever it happens, the basic problem is the same: children must learn to link the new written form of representation with the concrete understanding of number which they already have when they start school. They must learn, for example, that adding one brick to two bricks can be represented by '2 + 1 = 3' and, conversely, that the statement '3 − 2 = 1' can be represented concretely by the removal of two bricks from three bricks. To use the terminology introduced in the last chapter, children must learn to translate between their concrete understanding of number and the written symbolism of arithmetic.

One way of looking at children's ideas about written symbolism is to ask them to produce their *own* written representations of simple arithmetical concepts. For example, a child might be given pencil and paper, shown a number of objects, and asked to put something on the paper to show how many objects are present. Alternatively, additions and subtractions may be performed on the objects and the child asked to represent what has been done. Using this method with pre-school children will tell us what ideas they have about written symbolism before they are introduced to the conventional system in school. The same method can also be used with school-age children who have already been introduced to the conventional system: do they fully appreciate the relationship between these symbols and additions and subtractions involving *real* objects?

This chapter reports the interesting and unexpected answers to these questions provided by research carried out with young children in Edinburgh. We will look first at children's attempts to represent the number of objects in a group, and later at their attempts to represent simple additions and subtractions.

Children's representations of quantity

When I embarked upon this line of enquiry, I could find only one previous study which had done anything similar. In this study, Barbara Allardice (1977) had asked American children aged 3 to 7 years to write messages which Snoopy (a 'blindfolded' toy dog) would read later on. Using this method, she had elicited their spontaneous representations of quantity, addition and subtraction. Allardice reported that young children found quantity much easier to represent than addition and subtraction. She also reported that many children invented their own methods, but gave few specific illustrations.

I was interested by Allardice's findings and decided to see for myself how young British children responded in the same situation. At first my method was very similar to Allardice's: I used small bricks, and a toy panda called Chu-Chu was the recipient of the children's messages. Although this procedure elicited responses from the children, it seemed unnecessarily artificial and elaborate. I dispensed with Chu-Chu and simply asked the children to 'put something on the paper' to show how many bricks were present, or what had happened to the bricks. Most children responded readily to this request: a few were hesitant at first but, after some gentle encouragement and repetition of the question, they too produced marks on the paper.

At this point I was joined by Miranda Jones, a final-year student in the Psychology Department of Edinburgh University. On the strength of my pilot study we decided to carry out a large-scale study. We used ninety-six children (aged 3 years 4 months to 7 years 9 months) in four groups: twenty-four children at each educational level, from nursery class to class 3. Their school served a cross-section of the community and the children came from a variety of socio-economic backgrounds. The children in the pre-school group had received no formal instruction in arithmetic; the children in class 1 had started on simple sums, adding on 1 and 2; and the children in classes 2 and 3 worked on problems in written arithmetic almost daily (see figure 5.1).

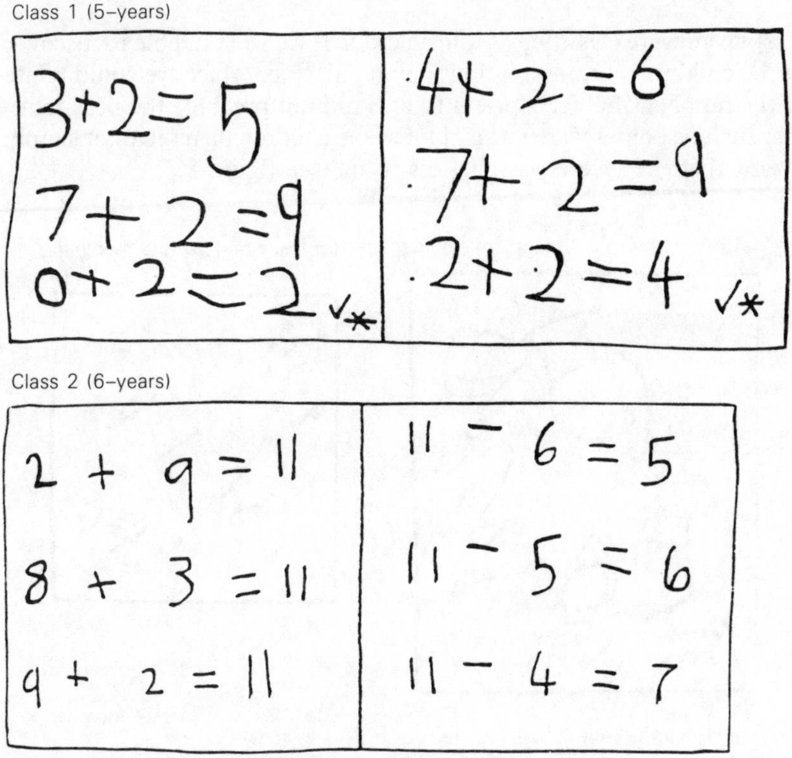

Class 1 (5–years)

$$3 + 2 = 5$$
$$7 + 2 = 9$$
$$0 + 2 = 2 \quad \checkmark*$$

$$4 + 2 = 6$$
$$7 + 2 = 9$$
$$2 + 2 = 4 \quad \checkmark*$$

Class 2 (6–years)

$$2 + 9 = 11$$
$$8 + 3 = 11$$
$$9 + 2 = 11$$

$$11 - 6 = 5$$
$$11 - 5 = 6$$
$$11 - 4 = 7$$

Figure 5.1   Pages from children's work-books.

Each child was seen individually by Miranda Jones, and was asked to represent the quantities one, two, three, five and six. They were presented with paper and pencil, and a quantity of bricks was placed on the table in front of them. They were then asked 'Can you put something on the paper to show how many bricks are on the table?' This particular wording was chosen as it did not mention either 'writing' or 'drawing', and so left open to the children as many options as possible. When they had 'put something on the paper' the bricks were removed, and a new set of bricks and a fresh piece of paper placed in front of them. (For more details, see Jones, 1981.)

The children used a variety of methods to represent the bricks. On closer examination, we found that we could fairly easily divide these responses into four main categories.

Idiosyncratic responses

Responses were classified as idiosyncratic if we were unable to discover in the children's representations any regularities which we could relate to the number of objects present. This did not preclude the possibility that such responses were meaningful to the children themselves: it simply meant that they were meaningless to us (see figure 5.2).

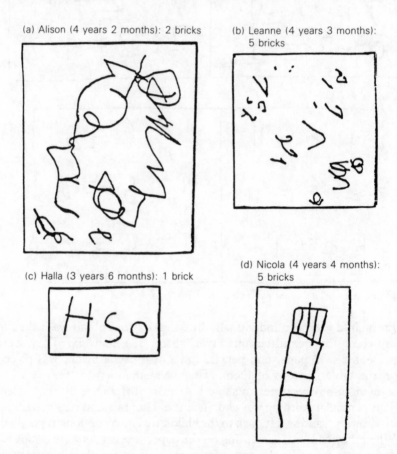

(a) Alison (4 years 2 months): 2 bricks

(b) Leanne (4 years 3 months): 5 bricks

(c) Halla (3 years 6 months): 1 brick

(d) Nicola (4 years 4 months): 5 bricks

Figure 5.2   Examples of idiosyncratic responses

The most common idiosyncratic response was simply to cover the paper with scribble, as in Alison's representation of two bricks. Some children, however, did not draw a continuous scribble on the paper, but made discrete letter-like squiggles. For example, Leanne actually said, 'I'm doing writing', as she very carefully made her marks on the paper. A third kind of idiosyncratic response was to produce recognisable letters of the alphabet, as illustrated by Halla. Finally, some children simply drew pictures of irrelevant objects, as in Nicola's drawing which she claimed to be of a chair.

Pictographic responses

'Pictographic' is a term often used to describe certain writing systems used in other cultures. The criterion here is that the children should be trying to represent something of the appearance of what was in front of them, as well as its numerosity. A response would be categorised as pictographic if the child incorporated within it an indication of the shape, position, colour or orientation of the bricks (see figure 5.3).

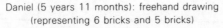

Daniel (5 years 11 months): freehand drawing
(representing 6 bricks and 5 bricks)

Rachel (4 years 10 months): draws round 6 bricks

Figure 5.3   Examples of pictographic responses

The most common pictographic response was simply to draw the bricks freehand, as Daniel attempted to do. A few children such as Rachel, however, placed each brick in turn on the paper and drew round it. This may have been a literal response to the instruction: 'Put something on the paper', with the child actually putting the brick on the paper rather than a mark, as we had intended! Alternatively, it could have been an aid to accuracy: one child drew the bricks freehand when the numbers involved were small, but placed them on the paper and drew round them for larger numbers.

Iconic responses

Like pictographic responses, these are based on one-to-one correspondence, but here the child uses a system whereby a discrete mark of their own devising represents each brick. Iconic responses usually took the form of simple tallies, as produced by Mutale (see figure 5.4). Occasionally, however, children drew other shapes to represent each brick, such as Emma who drew circles, and Pamela who drew houses.

Mutale (4 years 3 months): 5 bricks

Emma (5 years 2 months): 6 bricks

Pamela (5 years 1 month): 3 bricks

Figure 5.4   Examples of iconic responses

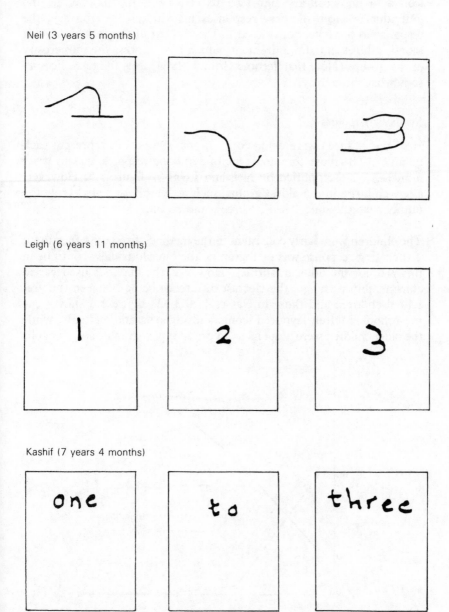

Figure 5.5 *Examples of symbolic responses (all representing 1, 2 and 3 bricks)*

The term 'iconic' as used here satisfies Charles Peirce's notion of an icon as a non-arbitrary sign (see Lyons, 1977, p. 102). While the individual *elements* of these responses may indeed be arbitrary, the response as a whole, considered in the context of the task, is not. It satisfies the essential requirement, which is to express the numerosity of the group. (Note that Jerome Bruner (1964) uses the term 'iconic' somewhat differently.)

Symbolic responses

Here the children were using conventional symbols to represent each quantity. The most common type of symbolic response was to write numerals, as exemplified by Neil and Leigh in figure 5.5. However, a few children in the oldest group, such as Kashif, actually wrote the number words 'one', 'two', 'three', and so on.

The children were fairly consistent in the method of response they used: if their first response was pictographic they would usually continue in this way for the other quantities. However, the methods used varied considerably with age, the clearest difference being between the pre-school children and those in classes 1 to 3. As figure 5.6 shows, the pre-school children favoured iconic and idiosyncratic methods, while the older children were more likely to produce pictographic and symbolic

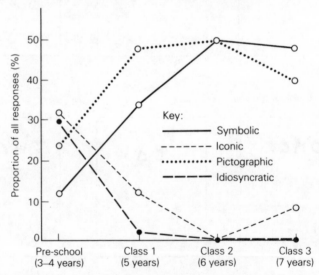

Figure 5:6   Type of response: variation with age

responses. It was not until class 3, however, that the conventional symbolic methods taught in school became the children's most common response.

We had expected that many pre-school children would produce idiosyncratic responses if they did not understand the nature of the task, or if they were unable to think of a way to respond. We had not, however, anticipated so many iconic responses amongst these youngest children. Like symbolic responses, iconic representations at first sight seem relatively abstract: they contain no information about the type of object being represented, and focus entirely on number. They seem in fact to be representing a very fundamental property, namely whether an object is present or absent. Indeed, the use of tallies here resembles the widespread use of fingers to represent objects (or people, etc.) which we saw in chapters 3 and 4. This similarity between tallies and fingers makes the frequency of iconic responses in the pre-school group less surprising.

The fact that the children produced a representation of the number of bricks does not necessarily mean that this representation was accurate. The children sometimes miscounted the bricks and so represented the wrong amount, or lost one-to-one correspondence. The children were more likely to be accurate with small numbers (1, 2 and 3) than with larger numbers (5 and 6) and, not surprisingly, the older children were more accurate than the younger ones.

Any mode of representation, if used systematically, can be considered an acceptable written representation of number – it is even possible that a child might construct an idiosyncratic system, meaningful to them alone, although none of the children in this study appeared to do so. Where the different methods diverge is in the *way* they convey information about number, and in the amount of additional information provided. Pictographs, for example, are useful in that they provide information not only about number, but also about other properties (size, shape, colour perhaps) of the objects being represented. An iconic system of tallies, on the other hand, tells us nothing about the objects but is often the most appropriate system for keeping track of events (this is discussed in more detail in the next chapter).

This property of iconic systems was nicely demonstrated by a girl called Lindsay (4 years 7 months) who in fact had taken part in my pilot study. Unlike the children in our main study, Lindsay used the same piece of paper throughout. I placed bricks on the table in front of her, one at a time, until there were seven altogether. As each brick was produced, Lindsay responded with a single vertical tally. I wanted to see how she would react when the bricks were being removed, and so I started taking them away, again one at a time. Lindsay's response was to put one small dot under a tally for each brick that was taken away. We ended up with no bricks on the table and the pattern of lines and dots shown in figure 5.7.

Figure 5.7   Creative iconic responses by Lindsay (4 years 7 months)

A symbolic system is usually the most efficient way of representing number, but does not ordinarily convey other information about the objects being represented. However, Juliette (3 years 10 months), another child from our pilot study, found an ingenious way round this problem. Despite her youth, Juliette was using a symbolic system in a systematic and regular way – she used a '1' for one brick, a backwards '2' for two bricks, a '3' for three bricks and so on. One of the drawbacks of a symbolic system is that it does not represent the position of objects, and so I wondered what Juliette would do if I put the three bricks in a tower. She responded by writing the numerals '1', '2', '3' in a vertical pattern. I then added two more bricks to the tower. Juliette pointed out that there was no room on her paper to add any more numbers on top of her previous pattern, so she wrote the '4' and '5' in a new vertical pattern, next to her old one, as shown in figure 5.8. Juliette showed great ingenuity in adapting her symbolic system to incorporate both iconic and pictographic elements.

Children's representation of zero

One problem facing any system of representation is how to represent the *absence* of quantity, or 'none'. To find out how the children would cope with this problem, the table was cleared of bricks and each child

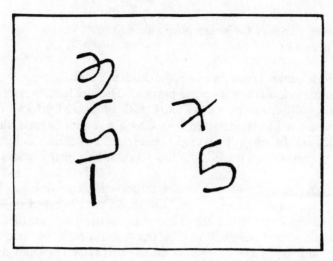

Figure 5.8   Creative symbolic responses by Juliette (3 years 10 months)

was asked, 'Can you now show that there are no bricks on the table?'

As expected, virtually all the children who used symbolic methods to represent quantity also used the conventional symbol '0' to represent the absence of bricks. There were, however, some idiosyncratic versions of this, as when Nicola (5 years 6 months) wrote '10', and said with satisfaction, 'That's what you put when there's none, eh?' Children who elsewhere had used iconic and pictographic methods responded in a variety of ways. Some also used the conventional symbol '0', or invented their own symbols such as a dot or dash. Others drew an empty box or table. Some of the children drew a single brick or tally. Finally, some children left the paper blank, and it was often hard to decide whether they did this deliberately to represent 'nothing' or whether they were simply unable to respond.

Unlike the previous questions, we found that many children responded to the problem of representing 'nothing' with puzzled looks, and clearly found it hard to understand what we were asking them to do. We were made very aware that, in general, they had been given no rationale at all for making these marks on paper: their representations served no obvious purpose for anyone concerned. On the whole this did not seem to have inhibited them from putting pen to paper – in fact we had elicited a wide range of interesting responses from the children. Nevertheless it still raised the question of what meaning, if any, these responses actually held for the children themselves.

Producing symbols for some purpose:
The Tins game

I decided to devise a game in which the children's written representations would serve a clear communicative purpose. The idea for this game arose fairly naturally from my earlier work with boxes and bricks. Young children seemed to be attracted by a closed box containing a number of bricks, and I thought they might be intrigued by the idea of putting a written message on the lid of a box to show how many bricks were inside.

The game centred on four identical tobacco tins, containing different numbers of bricks: usually there were three, two, one and no bricks inside each tin. After letting the child see inside the tins, I shuffled them around, and asked the child to pick out 'the tin with two bricks in', 'the tin with no bricks in' and so on. At this stage the child had no alternative but to guess. After a few guesses, I interrupted the game with 'an idea which might help'. I attached a piece of paper to the lid of each tin, gave the child a pen, and suggested that they 'put something on the paper' so that they would know how many bricks were inside. The children dealt with each tin in turn, its lid being removed so that they could see inside. When they had finished, the tins were shuffled around again, and the children were asked once more to identify particular tins and see whether their representations had 'helped them play the game'. The Tins game thus provided not only a clear rationale for making written representations, but also an opportunity to discover what children understood about what they had done.

I carried out a study in which I played the Tins game with twenty-five children, aged 3 years 1 month to 5 years 10 months. Fifteen of the children were in the nursery class and ten children in class 1 of a predominantly middle-class school. Each child was seen individually in a small room away from the classroom. (For more details, see Hughes and Jones, 1986.)

There was little doubt about the popularity of the game. The children found the initial guessing-game intriguing and were excited by the idea of making representations with paper and pencil. Several of their comments showed that they were very aware of how this could help them, such as: 'It's easy now coz I've done some writing.'

There was also little doubt that their representations did in fact help them play the game. Before they made their representations their ability to identify each tin was at chance level, but afterwards their performance was significantly higher: over two-thirds of the pre-school group and every child in class 1 was able to identify the tins from their representations.

What methods did the children use to represent the bricks? As before, their representations of non-zero quantities were categorised as idiosyncratic, pictographic, iconic or symbolic. Comparison with our earlier study showed that in many ways the children were responding in a similar fashion. In both studies the children produced a wide range of representations; in both studies the pre-school group produced high levels of idiosyncratic and iconic responses; and in both studies the class 1 group produced symbolic responses but no idiosyncratic responses. There were nevertheless two clear differences between the two studies.

The first difference concerned the children's representation of zero. In our earlier study, the request to show that there was nothing on the table had led to several puzzled looks. In the Tins game, representing the fact that there was nothing in a tin was treated just as straightforwardly as the other representations. The most common response in the pre-school group was to deliberately leave the paper blank (often accompanied by comments such as 'I'll no put any writing on there coz there's no bricks in the box'), while in the class 1 group the majority of children used the conventional zero. Other children produced a dash, as did Anna (figure 5.9), or drew an empty tin.

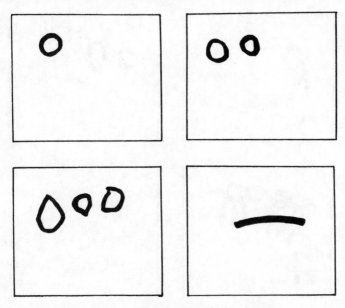

Figure 5.9   Representations of 1, 2, 3 and 0 bricks by Anna (4 years 0 months)

Anna's response raises the question of whether the children did in fact regard their representation of zero in the same light as their other representations. They might well have realised that they could identify the empty tin by default: that is, having identified the others as containing definite quantities of bricks, they would know that the remaining tin contained nothing. This possibility cannot be ruled out, although there was no sign that the children regarded the representation of 'no bricks' as any different from the other representations.

The second difference between this study and our previous one lay in the number of pictographic responses. This type of response – drawing round the bricks or, more commonly, drawing them freehand – was the most frequent overall response in our earlier study. In the Tins game, however, very few of the pre-school responses were pictographic, and none at all from class 1. This is presumably because in the Tins game the children knew that they had only to discriminate between different *numbers* of bricks, and were more focused on doing that successfully: an impulse to represent other features of the bricks or tins was much less likely to arise.

It is of course possible to represent the number of bricks in the tins by drawing the appropriate number of any object whatsoever. Some of the children seemed to be aware of this fact. Thus Shona (figure 5.10)

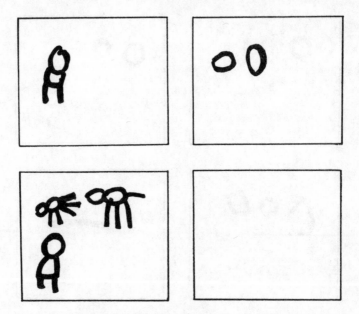

Figure 5.10   Representations of 1, 2, 3 and 0 bricks by Shona (4 years 4 months)

spent some time deciding what objects she would draw to represent the bricks: she finally decided on 'a girl' for one brick, 'two balls' for two bricks, and 'a girl and two doggies' for three bricks. For the empty tin she deliberately left the paper blank.

This kind of responding was most evident in the class 1 group, where it was produced by four of the ten children. One of these, Fiona (5 years 0 months), stared out of the window for a long time as if searching for inspiration: she eventually drew one tree, two houses and three doors – all of which were visible through the window (see figure 5.11).

Figure 5.11 Representations of 1, 2, 3 and 0 bricks by Fiona (5 years 0 months)

A different solution was adopted by Aaron (Figure 5:12). He was a great 'Star Wars' fan, and his representations consisted of 'a spaceship – it's a Tie fighter' for one brick and 'an elephant and a Walker' for two bricks. For three bricks he drew 'three spaceships – these two guys at the rear are coming after the front guy – that's fire coming out of the back.' Having done his drawings he then added the numerals '1', '2' and '3' to help him remember!

Figure 5.12 Representations of 1, 2, 3 and 0 bricks by Aaron (5 years 6 months)

Children whose representations were easily recognisable by an adult – such as Aaron, Fiona, Shona or Anna – were generally successful themselves at identifying the tins. In contrast, children whose responses were categorised as idiosyncratic nearly always failed to recognise them. One example is Sarah (figure 5.13): she drew the same brick-like shape for each tin, which did not help her identify the contents.

There were, however, some interesting exceptions to this. One was Richard, who produced one tally for one brick, two tallies for two bricks and three tallies for three bricks. For the empty tin he also produced a single tally, as shown in figure 5.14. When asked to identify these representations later, he showed no confusion at all between the empty tin and the tin containing one brick, 'That's got none in,' he said, pointing to the empty tin. 'How do you know?' I asked. Richard pointed to the little sideways line at the bottom of the tally: 'Coz this one's got a tail on, so it's got none in.'

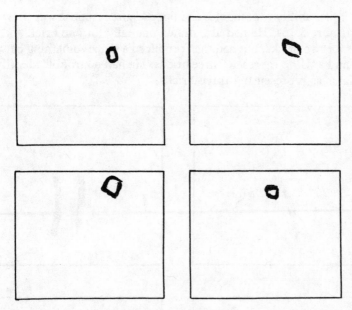

Figure 5.13   Representations of 1, 2, 3 and 0 bricks by Sarah (4 years 0 months): first session

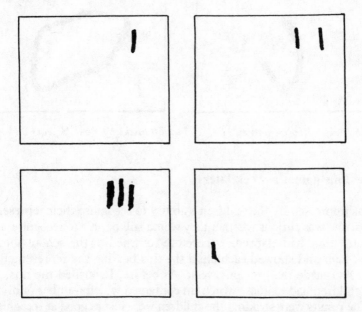

Figure 5.14   Representations of 1, 2, 3 and 0 bricks by Richard (4 years 2 months)

A similar ability to recognise an idiosyncratic response was shown by Paul (figure 5.15). He had also drawn one tally for one brick and two tallies for two bricks, but had then produced a shape something between a 'C' and a 'U' to represent three bricks. He had no trouble identifying this later as representing three bricks.

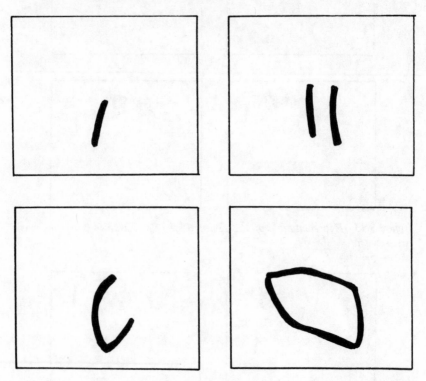

Figure 5.15   Representations of 1, 2, 3 and 0 bricks by Paul (3 years 8 months)

The Tins game: a week later

I was impressed by the children's ability to recognise their representations, and was curious whether they would still be able to recognise them if some time had elapsed. I therefore returned to the school about a week later and showed each child the tins bearing the representations they had made the previous week. As before, I shuffled the tins, and the children had to guess which tin contained which number of bricks.

The results were striking: the children were just as good at recognising their representations a week later as they had been at the time. Those children – such as Sarah – who had made idiosyncratic representations and had been unable to recognise them during the first session, were also unable to recognise them a week later. On the other hand, both Richard and Paul were still able to recognise their idiosyncratic representations a week later, with Richard again spontaneously referring to the 'tail' on his representation of zero.

I also used this second visit to the school to find out whether those children who had initially produced any unrecognisable idiosyncratic representations would benefit from the chance to have another go. These children – there were seven, all in the pre-school group – were first asked: 'Would you like to try it again?' Most of the children simply responded by saying they couldn't or wouldn't think of another way to do it, while those who did try again were no more successful than before. I then suggested the idea of one-to-one correspondence by saying, for example, 'Why don't you make two marks on the tin with the two bricks in?' The response to this was immediate. Five of the seven adopted the iconic strategy at once from a single example, generalising without further suggestions to the remaining tins. One of these five was Sarah, who had produced the four brick-like shapes shown in figure 5.13, and whose second attempt is shown in figure 5.16. The other two children

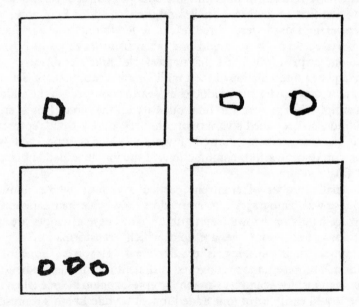

Figure 5.16   Representations of 1, 2, 3 and 0 bricks by Sarah (4 years 3 months): second session.

required further examples, but they too eventually adopted the rule. All these children were then able to identify their responses correctly. Thus, by the end of the study, all twenty-five children had produced recognisable sets of responses, with or without prompting.

Children's representation of addition and subtraction

The children studied by Miranda Jones and myself, referred to earlier in this chapter, were not only asked to represent quantities of bricks, but were also asked to represent simple additions and subtractions performed on the bricks. We had anticipated that this would be harder than representing quantities, but thought that the children might produce some interesting inventions, as they had when asked to represent quantity. We also expected that the older children would use the conventional symbols ' + ', ' − ' and ' = ' which they regularly used in school.

We used two tasks to elicit children's representations of addition and subtraction. In the first, known as the 'Complete Operations' task, the initial quantity had to be represented as well as what was done to it. In a typical version of this task, Miranda Jones would place two bricks on the table in front of the child and add two more, saying: 'Can you show that first we had two bricks and then we added two more?' The other versions used were: three bricks added to one brick, five added to six, five taken from six and one taken from three.

To our surprise, we found that not a single child was able to produce an adequate representation of these additions and subtractions. The most common response by far, produced by nearly two-thirds of the children, was simply to represent the final quantity on the table. However, the children also produced a variety of other responses: some represented the initial amount, some showed the amount added or subtracted, while others produced various combinations of the initial, added/subtracted, and final amounts.

A small number of children, particularly those whose dominant response was pictographic, attempted to show what had happened by drawing hands or arrows (see figure 5.17). These attempts are quite ingenious, and, once we are told which transformation is being attempted, their meaning is usually clear. However, none of the children's representations conveyed sufficient information to be totally unambiguous: for example, Rosanne's representation of 'one taken from three' could easily be of 'one added to two', while Leigh's representation of 'two added to two' could easily be of 'two added to four' or 'two taken from six'.

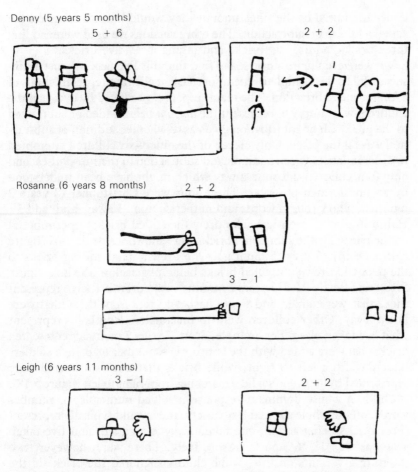

Figure 5.17   Attempts to represent addition and subtraction in Complete Operations task

The second task we used, known as the 'Pile' task, was intended to be much simpler. In a typical version of this task a large pile of about twenty-five bricks was placed on the table in front of the child. This time Miranda Jones said: 'Here's a big pile of bricks. I want you to show what I do to the pile. The first thing I'm going to do is this.' She would then, for example, take a brick from the pile and continue: 'Can you show that I took one brick away?' If the child began to count the pile, Miranda would say: 'No, don't count the bricks. I'm not interested in how many there are. I just want you to show what I did to the pile.' We hoped that by denying the children the opportunity to represent either the initial or the final amount they would have to focus on the actual addition or subtraction. The other versions we used were: adding three bricks, adding six bricks and taking away five bricks.

We were even more surprised to find that this Pile task was just as unsuccessful as the Complete Operations task at eliciting representations of addition and subtraction. The main response, produced by over half the children, was simply to represent the *amount* being added or subtracted to the pile, with no information given as to whether addition or subtraction was taking place. Only eleven of the ninety-six children attempted to differentiate between addition and subtraction in their responses, and only four children did so in a way which might have been understood by an uninformed observer. These four were Christopher (7 years 2 months), who wrote in words and numerals 'took 1 away' and 'add 3'; Habib (6 years 5 months), who drew the added bricks superimposed on the pile while the subtracted bricks were shown inside the box (figure 5.18); Denny (5 years 5 months), who drew a hand adding bricks to the pile, and drew subtracted bricks being put back in the box (figure 5.18); and finally Alec (5 years 2 months), who drew bricks to represent those that were added and wrote dashes to represent those that were taken away. Other children went to imaginative lengths to represent what had taken place. For example, Scott (7 years 7 months) represented bricks that were added with the appropriate number of British soldiers marching from left to right, while bricks that were subtracted were represented by Japanese soldiers marching from right to left (figure 5.18).

Children whose dominant response involved numerals, or number words, on the whole showed less variety: they would typically represent three bricks being added, one taken away, six added, and five taken away, as '3', '1', '6' and '5' respectively. There were, however, two interesting variants on this. Some children ignored the bricks in the pile and treated the four operations as a cumulative calculation: thus the sequence above would be represented as '3', '2', '8' and '3'. Others chose an arbitrary number for the contents of the pile and then performed a cumulative addition or subtraction on this number: they would thus produce a sequence such as '53', '52', '58' and '53'.

In contrast to all this ingenuity, *not a single child* on either the Complete Operations or the Pile task used the conventional operator signs ' + ' and ' – ' to represent addition and subtraction. This is particularly striking when it is recalled that, apart from those in the pre-school group, all the children in the study were using the formal symbolism of arithmetic every day in their work-books (see figure 5.1). These children clearly did not regard these symbols as relevant to the problems facing them. We had anticipated that the children would not find it easy to

Denny (5 years 5 months)

Habib (6 years 5 months)

Scott (7 years 7 months)

Figure 5.18 Attempts to represent addition and substraction in Pile task

represent addition and subtraction, but we had certainly not expected this universal reluctance to use the symbols of school arithmetic.

Finding a purpose for representing addition and subtraction

One possibility which required serious consideration was that the children would produce more successful representations of addition and subtraction if there was a clearer rationale or purpose for doing so. Accordingly, I tried to devise a game similar to the Tins game, in which the children had to represent on top of a tin whatever addition or subtraction had been performed on the contents. This turned out to be unexpectedly difficult: as before, the children were fixated on the *result* of the transformation, and almost invariably attempted to represent the *final amount* in the tin.

A different approach to this same problem was adopted by Miranda Jones. In a further study (Jones, 1982) she set up a communication task in which two children were seated on opposite sides of a screen, each with a collection of bricks. The children were given two different problems in which they had to send written messages to the other child. It was intended that both problems would require the children to represent additions and subtractions on paper. The children in this study were aged 5 to 9 years.

The first problem started with a tower of four bricks being built in front of one child. This child was asked to communicate enough information to enable the other child to build a tower of exactly the same height. Miranda Jones then took bricks off (or added them to) the tower, and asked the first child to convey information about this to the other child: 'Now I'm going to do something to your tower. I might put some more bricks on it, or I might take some away, and you have to send a message to (the other child) so that he can do the same to his tower.'

This difference in her procedure in fact had very little effect on the children's representations. As before, most of the children could represent quantities, but few of them managed to represent addition and subtraction. Again, the most common response was simply to describe the final result of the operation, either in numerals (e.g. '7') or in words ('I have 7 bricks now'). Very few of the children's responses actually described the operations carried out on the tower, and all of these used ordinary language (e.g. 'add 3 on top' or 'take away 2 from 5') rather than the conventional symbols of arithmetic.

Such symbols may in fact have been unnecessary, for there seemed to be a prevailing assumption amongst the children that messages consisting of a single number showed the final number in the tower. One pair of 7-year-olds, however, showed a systematic failure of communication. Paul would write, for example, 'put five bricks' (meaning five bricks in total), which Leila took to be an instruction to add five bricks to those already there. Too much information was the source of a misunderstanding between two 9-year-olds: Gareth, with a tower of four bricks in front of him, wrote: 'four bricks in a pile, one on top of another', but Catriona interpreted the message as an instruction to place one set of four bricks on top of another set of four.

The other problem which the children received was a 'communication' version of the Pile task. They each started with a large pile of bricks in front of them. Miranda Jones then took bricks off one child's pile, or added more to it; this child's task was to send a message to the other child so that she could do the same to her pile. In this case, as in the Pile task, it was not possible to represent the final quantity, as the number of bricks in each pile was not known.

As before, this difference in procedure had little effect, the most common response being simply to represent the *amount* that had been added or taken away. Only one child used conventional operator signs ('+' and '–') and she used them idiosyncratically: thus she wrote '4 – 4 = ' for the four-added item and '6 + 6 = ' for the six-taken item. Her partner was unable to interpret her messages correctly. Other responses ranged from the succinct 'take 1 away' to the garrulous 'Put four blocks on your hand from the box and then put them on the blocks already out, like this' (followed by a diagram). Thus, while this communication task was slightly more successful at eliciting adequate representations of addition and subtraction, it was no more successful at getting the children to use the conventional symbols of arithmetic.

Overview

This chapter has described in detail a number of studies carried out in Edinburgh in which young children were asked to represent quantities, or changes involving quantities, using pencil and paper. These findings not only confirm the earlier study of American children by Barbara Allardice (1977), but have themselves been confirmed by several other studies carried out since in different parts of the world: these include three studies of Swiss children (Schubauer-Leoni and Perret-Clermont, 1980); Sinclair, Siegrist and Sinclair, 1983; and Sinclair, 1984), a study of Australian children (Litwin, 1984), and a further study of Scottish children (Potts, 1983). These researchers all used slightly different tasks and had different questions in mind, but nevertheless the overall picture emerging is remarkably coherent.

First, it is now clear that even pre-school children are able to represent small quantities, either spontaneously, or with a small amount of prompting. Their representations are based primarily on one-to-one correspondence (that is, they are pictographic or iconic). The clearest demonstration of this comes from the Tins game, where children do not merely produce isolated responses, but rather generate coherent *systems* of notation.

Secondly, most children of this age can also represent zero. Despite frequent claims that the concept of zero is inherently difficult, the children studied here do not appear to have particular difficulty with the idea. Again, this is most clearly demonstrated in the Tins game, where children have to identify an empty tin by means of a representation on the lid. In this study, zero was no harder to represent than the quantities one, two or three.

Thirdly, in contrast to their readiness to represent quantity, even children as old as 9 have difficulty in representing the operations of addition and subtraction. Where possible, they will instead represent a quantity – usually the final result rather than the quantity added or subtracted. In tasks such as the Pile task, where they are unable to represent the final quantity because it is unknown, they will represent the quantity added or subtracted, but will give no information about the direction.

Finally, several of these studies show a striking reluctance on the part of school-age children to use the conventional operator signs of arithmetic. This is particularly puzzling, given that they find addition and subtraction generally hard to represent: one might well have expected them to be more ready to use signs whose specific purpose is to represent these very operations. It is even more puzzling when one knows that the Edinburgh children at least used these signs daily in their school work.

These findings have a number of important implications (which we will take up again later) concerning the way we introduce written symbolism. In particular, they point to a serious mismatch between the system of symbols which children are required to learn, and their own spontaneous conceptualisations. With regard to the representation of quantity, it seems that children themselves tend to use methods based on one-to-one correspondence, but are required to use a symbolic system instead. With regard to the representation of addition and subtraction, the problem is of a completely different order. It seems that the *whole notion* of representing these transformations on paper is something which children find very hard to grasp, although the exact reason for this difficulty is not yet entirely clear. Nevertheless, from an early age, children are being introduced to symbols ('+' and '–') which are intended to serve this purpose. This goes some way to explaining why children's understanding of these symbols does not go beyond the context in which they are taught. There appears to be a serious and disturbing split between their use of symbols in the classroom and their ability to apply them to problems encountered elsewhere.

6

The written number systems
of other cultures

Many of the children's inventions described in the last chapter bring
to mind the written number systems used by earlier cultures. The rows
of vertical tallies, the use of a dot for zero or the imaginative use of hands
to represent addition and subtraction seem almost as if they might belong
in the paintings of early cave dwellers, or on the tablets of ancient
Egyptian scribes. This suggests the intriguing possibility that, unknown
to them, the children were using fundamental and universal methods
of representation.

The idea that aspects of children's development should be parallel
to the evolution of the human species is by no means new. Expressed
in the form 'ontogeny recapitulates phylogeny' – that is, development
within an individual (ontogeny) will both mirror and incorporate the
development of the species (phylogeny) – it has been the cause of much
debate amongst biologists and geneticists. This idea also formed a promi-
nent part of Piaget's interest in genetic epistemology, and he himself
pointed out interesting similarities and dissimilarities between the
evolution of geometrical thinking and the development of geometrical
ideas in the child. To the best of my knowledge, though, no one has
yet compared children's inventions of written symbolism with the
development of written notation in earlier cultures.

Unlike Piaget, my intention in making such a comparison is not to
develop a global theory concerning the development of knowledge: as
we shall see, the evolution of written number systems is sufficiently
diverse to make such an enterprise difficult, if not impossible. Rather
I am motivated by the idea that, if we look at the various ways in which
different people have tackled the same problem of representing number
in writing, and at the breakthroughs and pitfalls that attended the subsequent development of their number systems, we may find some clues

as to how best to teach present-day children to understand, appreciate and make use of our own system of written arithmetic.

This chapter therefore looks at ways in which other cultures have represented in writing the concepts of quantity, addition and subtraction. Since I am not myself a historian of mathematics, I have had to rely very much on other authorities. I have found Graham Flegg's *Numbers: Their History and Meaning* (1984) and Florian Cajori's *A History of Mathematical Notations* (1928) particularly useful.

Fingers

It seems likely that, long before people represented number in writing, they used the fundamental device of representing objects with their fingers. This device – which we have already seen being used by contemporary pre-school children and their mothers – seems so natural and obvious as to be quite unremarkable. Yet it is precisely because fingers are both natural and obvious that they have been used in so many different cultures. As Flegg points out (p. 14): 'The evidence of finger-counting is so widespread that we are forced to conclude that it has been a universal practice.'

Flegg suggests (p. 8) that fingers may well have been used as a method for comparing sets of objects, by people who were unable to count.

He could by now compare, for example, his sheep or cattle with his fingers and toes, one by one, and so find out if all his flock were remaining safe in his keeping. So, in the morning a man who had fifteen sheep (say) would see that his flock corresponded to two hands and one foot. If he made a similar comparison later in the day and found that he had more fingers and toes on his two hands and one foot than he had sheep, he would know that his flock was no longer complete, even when he was yet unable actually to count the number missing.

Flegg also points out that references to fingers are common in the early words used for numbers, particularly in phrases which describe raising or bending fingers. He gives as a typical example the following sequence of number-words (p. 10)

> the end one is bent;
> another is bent;
> the middle one is bent;
> one is still left;
> the hand has died.

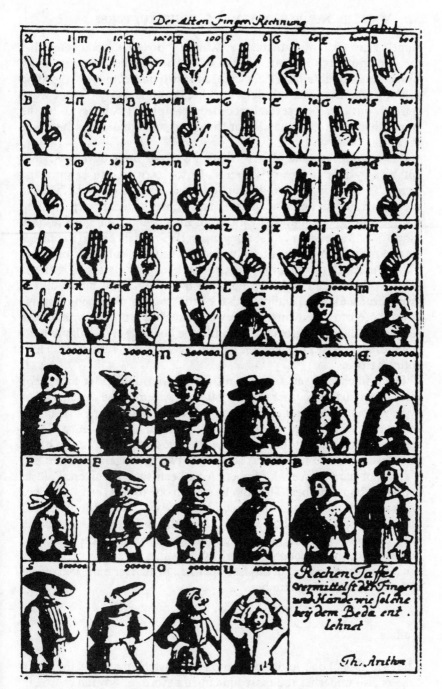

Figure 6.1 Bede's finger-counting
(Leupold, 1727, from Flegg, 1984, p. 15)

Another historian of mathematics, Walter Popp (1978), points out that the contemporary Botocudos tribe of Brazil use the words meaning 'finger' and 'double-finger' for 'one' and 'two' respectively. According to Popp, the Botocudos designate all larger numbers by the one word 'many', but there are several recorded examples of cultures using the words 'hand' and 'two-hands' for 'five' and 'ten', and even 'the whole man' for 'twenty'.

Finger-counting and finger-calculating have been developed into complex systems in many societies. In the early eighth century the Venerable Bede, in the introduction to a work describing how to calculate the dates for Easter, gave full details of a complex system for representing numbers up to one million by means of fingers and hand gestures (see figure 6.1). More recently, Geoffrey Saxe (1979) has described a complex system of representation currently used by the Oksapmin tribe of Papua New Guinea. In this method, the Oksapmin count by starting with the thumb of one hand and then pointing to twenty-seven places on the arms, head and body, ending with the little finger of the opposite hand. If they need to count further, they continue back up the wrist of the second hand and progress back around the body again (see figure 6.2). According to Saxe, this system is used for everyday activities such as counting pigs.

The influence of our fingers on the way we think about number is most clearly felt in the fact that our number system – like so many other systems – is based around the number ten. In fact, the great majority of systems which employ a base at all use five, ten or twenty. There seems little doubt that this is because we have five fingers on one hand, ten fingers on two hands and altogether twenty fingers and toes.

It is not hard to see why fingers have been such a universal aid in thinking about number. They can be used in one-to-one correspondence with an unlimited range of objects, they are easy to manipulate, and we take them with us wherever we go. Yet they have one disadvantage: they cannot be used to make an enduring record. As soon as human beings felt the need, not only to work out how many objects were present, but also to keep a record of this fact, they had to look for more permanent ways of representing number.

Tallies

The principle of one-to-one correspondence which underlies the use of fingers also underlies the most fundamental form of written representation, that of tallying. Tallies, as we have already seen, appear very

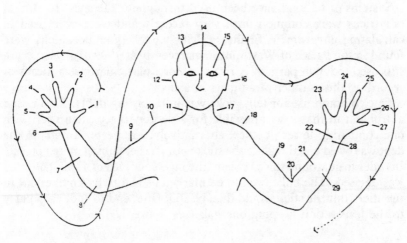

Figure 6.2   Oksapmin counting
(from Saxe, 1979, p. 39)

frequently in the spontaneous representations of young contemporary children. At the same time, tallying is one of the oldest methods known of representing number: markings on bones, knots tied in string and notches carved on sticks are amongst the most primitive representations found. As A. Hooper (1951) points out in *The River Mathematics* (p. 6):

> One cave dweller might keep a record of the number of enemies he slaughtered: another, higher-minded, would note down the number of times the puzzling phenomenon occurred that we now – incorrectly – call 'sunrise'. In any case each mark or cut would indicate the number one. Many ancient cave-dwellings still show such markings, the earliest attempts made by man to represent spoken numbers by written symbols. Such number-writings go back long before the invention of any other form of writing.

This method has indeed been traced back nearly 30,000 years. In 1937 a wolf-bone from the Palaeolithic period was discovered in Moravia (part of Czechoslovakia). The bone is about 18 cm long and has more than fifty notches cut into it. These are arranged in two series, with twenty-five notches in the first series and thirty in the second; within each series the notches are arranged in groups of five (see e.g. Flegg, 1984, pp. 41–2). This carving illustrates not only the extremely fundamental nature of tallying, but also the advantage of grouping tallies, with the unit of five again being the one preferred.

Systems of tallying have been used throughout the ages. In Britain tallysticks were common until very recently and were even used in calculating government finances: British Exchequer tallysticks were found in the Palace of Westminster as recently as 1909. Tallysticks are still used today in parts of Africa and Asia, particularly as a means of recording the number of animals in a flock.

One common use for tallysticks was in recording debts. This raised a problem in that it was possible for a debtor to replace a stick with one containing fewer notches; alternatively, the person to whom the debt was owed could replace the stick with one containing more notches. In order to get round this problem, the ingenious idea of a split tallystick was devised. The tallies would be marked as before by notches cut in the stick, but the stick would then be split from end to end, each party to the transaction keeping one half (see figure 6.3).

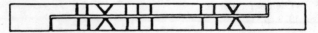

Figure 6.3   Split tallystick
(from Flegg, 1984, p. 44)

Tallying is particularly useful when keeping track of a series of events, especially if one does not know what the final total will be. A classic example is the cowboy adding a notch to his gun for each victim. A similar practice was adopted in World War II by fighter pilots, who would write symbols on the side of their planes to signify each enemy plane they had shot down. Prisoners may keep track of time by writing tallies on the walls of their cell – in this case the unit of grouping is usually seven, to mark the passage of a week.

Tallies are used in Britain today in many situations where we need to keep track of events (such as a batsman's runs in cricket), or to make an ongoing survey of specific occurrences (different kinds of vehicle on a particular stretch of road, for instance). They are usually grouped in fives, with the fifth tally being a diagonal stroke through the preceding four (ЦН). We also use tallies in some circumstances where a particular convention has been adopted: David Pimm has pointed out that the countdown signs to motorway turn-offs provide a good example of this – the sequence of signs is quite incomprehensible to a traveller who is ignorant of its meaning, despite its being founded on the universal principle of tallying.

Early developments from tallying

The principle of one-to-one correspondence thus forms the unifying link between the use of fingers, children's early attempts to represent number, and the idea of tallying. It also forms the basis of many of the earliest number systems, such as the Egyptian hieroglyphic system, the Babylonian cuneiform system and the more familiar Roman system.

The Egyptian hieroglyphic system has been traced back to 3300 BC and is found mainly on monuments of stone, wood or metal. Each quantity from one to nine was represented by the appropriate number of vertical strokes. These were usually grouped in threes or fours: thus 'five' would be represented by a row of three on top of a row of two, and eight by two rows of four (see figure 6.4, first column). The Egyptians had separate symbols for '10', '100', '1000', '10,000', '100,000' and '1,000,000'. The symbol for '10' was an inverted U-shape, so that '59' would be written

$$\cap\cap\cap \; ||| \\ \cap\cap \; ||| \\ |||$$

A similar system of notation was developed by the Babylonians. Their medium was clay: a wedge-shaped stylus was impressed on soft clay tablets which were then baked hard in ovens or in the heat of the sun. These were surprisingly enduring, and many have survived from almost 2000 BC to the present time. Like the Egyptians, the Babylonians had separate symbols for tens and units. A unit was usually represented by a thin vertical wedge-shape, while ten was represented by a broad sideways wedge. Thus '59' would be represented in the Babylonian system as

At the number 60, however, the Babylonian and Egyptian systems diverged, with the Babylonians employing the extremely useful idea of place-value. This exploits the fact that the same symbol can represent different numbers if one takes account of its position in a sequence. In the Babylonian system the symbol for '1', if written to the left of other larger symbols, would represent '60': thus

would now mean '81'.

Despite their many achievements, the Romans did not develop the idea of place-value as far as the Babylonians had done. As is well known,

the Roman system of numbers was also based on one-to-one correspondence of vertical strokes for the numbers one to four. It is possible
– as has frequently been suggested – that these Roman numerals originally represented fingers. Certainly the Latin word 'digitus' – from which
our modern word 'digit' derives – means 'finger'. It has also been
suggested that the Roman symbol for five, 'V', derives from the shape
of an open hand, with the thumb on one side and the four fingers grouped
together on the other, and that the symbol for ten, 'X', comes from
juxtaposing two 'V's. Later the Romans developed the idea of using
order to simplify their system. Thus, writing a smaller number to the
left of a larger one (as in 'IX') meant that the smaller number had to
be subtracted from the larger, whereas writing it to the right of the larger
number (as in 'XI') meant that it had to be added. Although this made
it simpler to write down numbers, it also meant that the value of the
number was not so immediately obvious. Thus '59' in the Roman system
would be written as 'LIX', which is much more opaque than its counter-
part in either the Egyptian or the Babylonian system.

The evolution of numerals

Systems such as the Egyptian and Babylonian, which depend very largely
on one-to-one correspondence, certainly have the advantage that they
are easy to understand. They are, however, extremely cumbersome,
particularly if every symbol has to be chiselled in wood or stone. It is
not surprising that these early systems were eventually replaced by
systems in which each number below the base of the system (that is,
the numbers one to nine in our own system) had its own unique symbol.
This process is known as *cipherisation*, and we can speak of our own
system as being fully cipherised. In contrast, the Babylonian and Egyptian systems are only partially cipherised, in that only a few numbers,
such as one and ten, have their own unique symbols.

The Egyptian hieroglyphic system in fact evolved into a more cipherised version between 3300 BC and 2000 BC. This newer version of
representation is called the *hieratic* script. According to Cajori, the hieratic
script was originally the result of writing hieroglyphics quickly, using
a reed pen on papyrus. It is interesting that 'hieratic' means 'priestly'
and that the hieratic script was very much the property of the priests.
Certainly the process of cipherisation makes numbers more obscure and
mysterious, and this fact could have been exploited by a particular group
such as the priests.

Around 800 BC a third form of Egyptian script evolved called the *demotic* or popular script. As figure 6:4 shows, the demotic symbols were an even more abbreviated version of the hieratic symbols, and these passed into popular use.

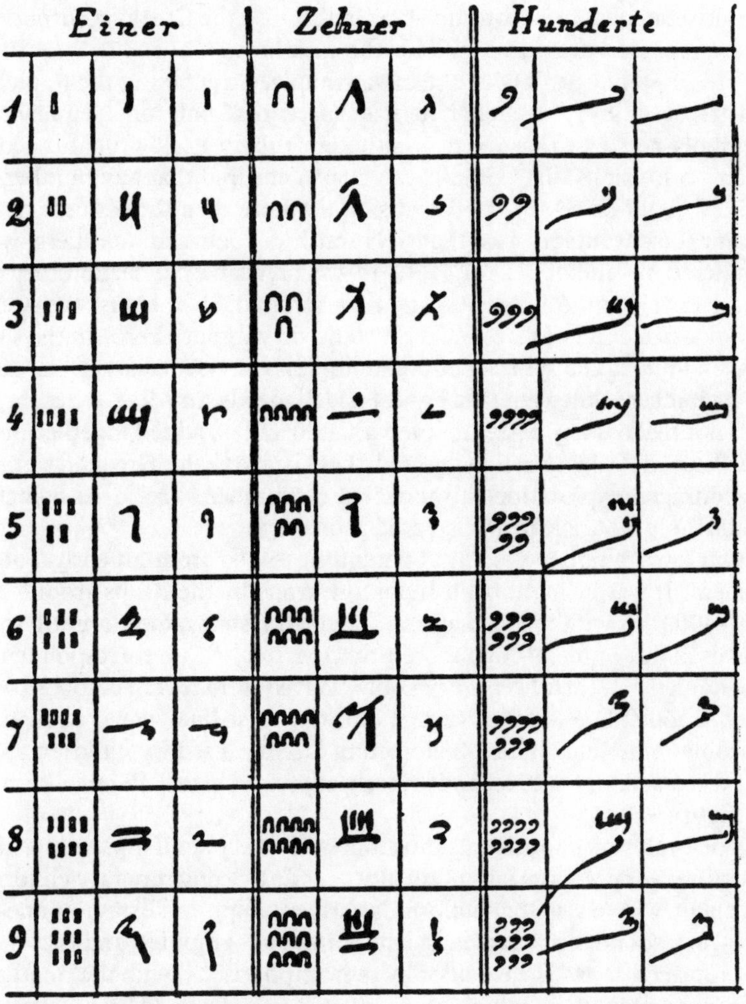

Figure 6.4   Egyptian hieroglyphic, hieratic and demotic number notations (by Kurt Sethe, from Cajori, 1928, p. 12)

The process of cipherisation took a rather different course in ancient Greece. At that time various Semitic races used the letters of their alphabets to represent numbers, and from about 500 BC onwards the

Greeks used a system based on this idea. In the Greek system, numbers from one to nine were represented by the first nine letters of the alphabet, the 'tens' from ten to ninety by the next nine, and the 'hundreds' from one hundred to nine hundred by the last nine letters. The Greek alphabet unfortunately only had twenty-four letters – so the Greeks incorporated three archaic letters to make up the numbers.

This system certainly had many advantages. By basing the numerals on the letters of the alphabet, it ensured that only one sequence of symbols needed to be learnt – although this in itself probably led to many confusions. The Greek system also ensured that any number up to 999 could be represented by using no more than three symbols. Its major disadvantage was that relationships between numbers were rendered opaque: for example, there was no visible connection between the numbers four (δ), forty (μ) and four hundred (υ) – because the system did not make use of place-value, it could do without a zero. In the same way, additions and subtractions of multiples bore no obvious resemblance to each other – knowing that 3 and 4 added together made 7, for example, did not make it any easier to know that 30 and 40 added together made 70. Indeed, it has been suggested that, because the Greek system so discouraged exploration in the world of number, Greek mathematics could only flourish in the area of geometry.

Our own number system apparently evolved from an early Hindu system. It was brought from India to Europe by the Arabs around AD 800–1000. As with the Roman and Egyptian systems, there are still some traces in our numerals of a more primitive one-to-one correspondence: the numerals '2' and '3' have possibly evolved from representations based on horizontal lines – when written quickly, these lines would easily have become joined up. This phenomenon is often used by children as an aid when adding on three, and is nicely expressed in the 'Peanuts' cartoon in figure 4.1.

The evolution of numerals thus followed a very similar pattern to that seen in the representations of quantity made by contemporary children. In chapter 5 we saw that children's early attempts are based on one-to-one correspondence (classed as iconic and pictographic), and that these are replaced as they grow older by more cipherised (symbolic) methods of representation, in which each quantity is represented by a separate symbol. The advantage of the latter – both for the children and for our ancestors – is that they are more efficient, and less cumbersome to write. However, this gain is accompanied by a corresponding loss in the ease with which they can be grasped by the uninitiated.

Place-value and zero

This parallel between the children's representations and those of early cultures does not seem at first sight to hold for zero. The zero symbol appeared relatively late in the evolution of number systems, and the concept itself has a reputation even in our culture for being hard to grasp. At the same time, our research using the Tins game (see chapter 5) revealed that contemporary young children are as adept at representing 'nothing' as they are at representing small quantities such as one, two and three.

This anomaly can perhaps be explained by distinguishing between two different uses of zero. The first and simpler use is that in which the symbol shows that there is no quantity present. Sometimes it will suffice to leave the paper blank, as was done by several of the children in chapter 5, but sometimes a symbol is necessary: we saw children as young as 3 years either using the conventional zero symbol or happily inventing symbols for themselves. It seems that this aspect of zero – representing the absence of quantity – is not particularly difficult to grasp.

Much more difficult is the use of zero in a place-value system. In such a system the quantity being represented by a particular symbol depends on the *position* of the symbol in a sequence. Thus the symbol '9' stands for nine in the number '59', but for ninety in the number '95'. This extremely useful idea of place-value means that any number, however large, can be represented by a relatively small set of numerals. Any system based on place-value, however, is faced with a problem: how to cope with a number like 'three hundred and four', where the 'tens' column is empty. The Babylonians, whose culture was the earliest to use place-value, first of all solved this problem by leaving an empty space. This sometimes led to confusion. For instance, the following symbol, $\prime\prime$ $\prime$, might have meant either $2(60) + 1$, or $2(60 \times 60) + 1$, bearing in mind that the Babylonian system was based around 60.

It seems that the early Babylonians (from 2000 BC to 1700 BC) must have relied on context to distinguish which meaning was intended. Records from the more recent Seleucid period (around 300 BC) suggest that the Babylonians later developed a zero symbol consisting of two small wedges placed diagonally. This symbol was used as a 'place-holder', to show that a column was empty. Thus $\prime\prime\text{\textbackslash}\prime$ would represent $2(60 \times 60) + 0(60) + 1$. This 'zero' was not, however, used on the right hand end of a number to show that the units column was empty. Again, we have to assume that the Babylonians relied on context to distinguish between '60' and '1'.

Cajori suggests that the Mayan civilisation of South America was probably the first to use both place-value and zero in a rigorously systematic fashion: this they achieved around the first century AD. The Maya used various symbols for zero, of which one resembles a half-closed eye. A more recent article in *Science* by H. R. Harvey and B. J. Williams (1980) suggests that the Aztec Indians also had a system which used both place-value and zero. The Hindu system, which is a direct ancestor of our own system, also incorporated the idea of place-value: it appears that this first occurred around 600 AD, but that it was another 200 years before there was evidence of a separate symbol for zero. Interestingly enough, this symbol was originally a dot, which was one of the zero symbols used by children in the last chapter. The logic of making as small a mark as possible to represent zero has apparently been followed, not only by the Hindus, but also by several contemporary African tribes (see Zaslavsky, 1973).

These developments suggest that one reason for the late appearance of zero was that it was only in a place-value system that a clear need for it arose. However, it still seems that the use of zero in such a system can cause difficulty. Flegg (1984, p. 72) argues that the take-up of the Hindu–Arabic system in western Europe was slow because the zero presented problems of comprehension: 'People found it hard to understand how it was that a symbol which stood for nothing could, when put next to a numeral, suddenly multiply its value ten-fold.' It seems likely that it is this kind of misunderstanding about the role of zero within a place-value system that causes difficulty, rather than the fact that it is a symbol which represents nothing.

Addition, subtraction and equality

As we have seen, contemporary young children have considerable difficulty in producing written representations of addition and subtraction. They also make surprisingly little use of the conventional operator signs ' + ', ' – ' and ' = '. Are there any parallels to this in the history of written number systems?

In accounts of the development of early number systems, representations of addition and subtraction are conspicuous by their absence. Most cultures developed a notation for representing quantities, but very few developed a notation for representing arithmetical operations. One of the main reasons for this is that many early calculations were not carried out in writing, but were performed on a device such as an abacus. Frequently, only the results of the calculation were written down.

Two early exceptions to this general rule were the Babylonians and the Egyptians. According to Cajori (1928, p. 6), the Babylonians used a particular juxtaposition of marks, ⌐ (the name of which has been transliterated as 'LAL'), for 'minus'. This symbol could be found within other symbols: thus all versions of the symbol for '19' were basically of the form '20 minus 1', with the sign for '1' enclosed or separated by the 'LAL' (figure 6.5).

Figure 6.5   Representation of '19' as '20 − 1' in Babylonian system (from Cajori, 1928, p. 6).

Signs for both addition and subtraction could be found in early Egyptian systems. Particularly interesting are symbols found in the Rhind papyrus which is dated about 1650 BC. In this papyrus, addition and subtraction are represented by pairs of walking legs (Cajori, 1928, pp. 229–30). It seems that legs walking from left to right represent addition, while those walking from right to left represent subtraction. There is an intriguing parallel here with 7-year-old Scott (see p. 74 and figure 5.18): this child used British soldiers marching from left to right to represent addition, while Japanese soldiers marching from right to left represented subtraction (see figure 6.6).

from Rhind papyrus, *c*. 1800 BC (taken from T. E. Peet by Cajori, 1928, p. 230).

by *Scott* (7 years 7 months)

Figure 6.6   Use of walking legs to represent addition and subtraction

The Alexandrian mathematician Diophantus (AD 250), who is often regarded as the father of algebra, invented his own sign ⋀ for subtraction. Like the Babylonians, he apparently did not require one for addition. It is interesting that his sign embodies an idea of movement or direction, and it will be recalled that several children in Chapter 5 used arrows in this way.

The modern ' + ' and ' − ' signs are comparatively recent. According to Cajori, they first came into use in Germany in the fifteenth century. Their exact meaning then, however, is not clear. Some sources claim that they were used in warehouses to signify quantities that were overweight (' + ') or underweight (' − '). An alternative explanation is that ' + ' derives from the Latin word *et*, meaning 'and', which was sometimes written in a form resembling a cross, e.g. ⤙. The sign for 'minus' might also have derived from Diophantus' sign ⋀, which subsequently evolved into ⊤.

Our own sign for 'equals' is also relatively recent, although it appears that the Egyptians had a symbol for the phrase 'it gives'. The modern equals sign was invented by Robert Recorde, who stated in a text published in 1557 that he would use the sign which he often used in his work: 'a paire of parallels. . .of one lengthe,. . .bicause noe 2. thynges, can be moare equalle.' Despite this self-contained explanation for the sign, it was apparently over one hundred years before it was accepted more generally. During this time Recorde's sign had to compete with other signs, including one used by Descartes (∝).

The evolution of signs to represent addition and subtraction thus shows a number of striking parallels with the children's own representations. In both cases we find a relative absence of representations for these operations, an early use of signs embodying movement and direction, and a relatively late introduction of conventional signs such as ' + ', ' − ' and ' = '.

The nature of written representation

There are undoubtedly some clear parallels between the development of children's representations of number and the evolution of the various systems of notation used by other cultures. They are both marked by an early and pervasive use of one-to-one correspondence, a gradual replacement with more efficient cipherised systems, and only a very late use of symbols for representing addition, subtraction and equality. At the same time, there is sufficient diversity − both in the children's representations and in the cultural systems − to show that human development does not follow a unitary path, and that ontogeny does not inevitably recapitulate phylogeny. We should instead be thinking more in terms of similar human responses to the problem of representing numerical information on paper. We should also not forget that the property of the medium itself, and the actions involved in using it, undoubtedly influence the possible solutions to this problem.

Consider first the nature of the medium. Marks on paper – or on stone – are essentially static, permanent records. Once made they are not easily changed. They thus lend themselves more readily to the representation of static quantities such as number than to the representation of dynamic operations such as addition and subtraction. Moreover, paper is a medium which allows information to be represented spatially: marks on paper can be arranged so that they resemble the spatial layout – and appearance – of the objects they represent. The nature of the medium thus tends to encourage pictographic and iconic systems. It seems that, using elaborations of such systems, early attempts to represent addition and subtraction involved the representation of dynamic properties of a *physical* kind, such as movement, direction or enclosure. The idea that a purely abstract mark on paper can represent a change or alteration of some kind does not, it seems, come at all easily.

An interesting demonstration of this point comes from a study carried out by Emilia Ferreiro (1978) on children's conceptions of the nature of writing. Ferreiro studied a group of Argentinian children aged 4 to 6 years, who had not yet been formally introduced to reading or writing. These children had very clear ideas about what parts of speech could or could not be represented on paper. In general, the idea that written words could represent nouns was accepted some time before the idea that they could represent verbs. For example, many children would argue that, in the sentence 'Daddy kicks the ball', the words 'Daddy' and 'ball' could be written down, but not 'kicks'.

We should also consider the physical action involved when written symbols are produced. A mark on paper is produced by a dynamic action, a movement of the hand and arm, yet the result of such an action is a static and relatively permanent entity. In the case of tallies, the action involved in making a downward stroke is very close to the action of reaching out and touching objects when counting them: they are both ways of 'marking off', which seems to be very fundamental. In contrast, the representation of dynamic actions requires first the inhibition of our own physical – or gestural – representation of that action. As Lev Vygotsky (1978) pointed out (p. 107):

A child who has to depict running begins by depicting the motion with her fingers, and she regards the resultant marks and dots on paper as a representation of running. When she goes on to depict jumping, her hand begins to make movements depicting jumps; what appears on paper remains the same. In general, we are inclined to view children's first drawings and scribbles rather as gestures than as drawing in the true sense of the word.

Overview

There are a number of fascinating parallels between the representations of young children and the systems developed by various other cultures. These parallels do not prove the idea that 'ontogeny recapitulates phylogeny', or suggest any general course which human evolution and development must inevitably follow: the evolution of number systems takes many forms and has developed into many backwaters and blind alleys. Rather, it seems that there are important similarities in the ways in which people in different situations cope with the problem of pro-ducing written representations of number and arithmetical operations.

There is, at the same time, considerable variety in the different number systems invented by human beings. There is an important point here for the way we teach children mathematics. It is usually implicit in the way we teach children that our own number system is the only possible way of representing basic arithmetical operations. Yet clearly this is not true. There is much that children could gain from learning about systems other than our own, and from considering the advantages and dis-advantages of different systems. In understanding how our current system has evolved, they may come to see its purpose and value more clearly.

Detailed study of the evolution of number systems also suggests that there is often a trade-off between efficiency and comprehension. There is little doubt that the system we currently use is an extremely efficient and powerful tool, the result of a long period of development. However, this increase in power and efficiency has been achieved by incorporating features – such as fully cipherised numerals, place-value and operator signs – which do not feature naturally in the representations of young children. As a result, we would expect that the highly condensed way in which addition and subtraction is represented (e.g. '3 + 4 = 7') will present considerable difficulties for young children. In the next chapter we will look at whether this is so.

7

Understanding the written symbolism of arithmetic

The children studied in chapter 5 revealed a striking reluctance to use the conventional symbolism of arithmetic (such as '1 + 3' or '− 5') to represent concrete additions and subtractions carried out with bricks. These children clearly did not regard the arithmetical symbolism which they used daily in the classroom as relevant to these new problems with which they were suddenly confronted. In one sense this is understandable, as the tasks they were attempting were very different from the contexts in which children learn arithmetical symbolism in school. At the same time, a genuine understanding of the meaning of arithmetical symbols should surely involve a readiness to apply these symbols to a wide range of concrete situations, to translate easily and fluently between the written and the concrete. Instead, there seemed to be a large gap between the children's concrete numerical understanding and their use of formal written symbolism.

In this chapter we will look at this gap from a different point of view, by considering what is known about children's *understanding* of written arithmetical symbolism. Our concern here is not with whether children can manipulate these symbols – that is, whether they can successfully carry out conventional 'sums' – or even with whether they can recognise numerals and operator signs and give their correct names. Rather, our interest is in what children understand these signs to mean, and whether they can demonstrate this understanding to others.

Numbers in the environment

The conventional arithmetical symbolism currently taught in school involves two main elements: the representation of quantity by numerals

('1', '2', '3', etc.) and the use of operator signs ('+', '−', '=', etc.) to represent transformations on these quantities and relationships between them. These two elements are by no means equally familiar to young children. Numerals are widely used in our environment for a variety of different purposes, and long before they start school children may become very familiar with the appearance of written numbers. In contrast, even the most common operator signs '+' and '−' are rarely found in children's ordinary environment. Indeed, these signs are more frequently encountered in situations where no arithmetical information is intended, as, for example, the cross on the side of an ambulance.

Numerals are used in our environment to convey a wide range of different types of numerical information. Sometimes they convey information about quantity, the number of objects in a group: 'This packet contains 6 fish fingers', '4 bottles of milk today please'. Sometimes they are used to order a sequence, as in the numbering of pages, or of houses in a street. Sometimes they convey information about price, or about identity (as on a car number-plate), or about a restriction (such as the number of passengers allowed to stand in a bus). It is often implicitly assumed that people will know which particular use is intended, and will not, for instance, believe that behind a door with '1' on it lives somebody all alone.

Little research has been done on the interesting question of how young children come to understand the different ways in which numbers are used in their environment. One exception is a study recently carried out in Geneva by Anne and Hermine Sinclair (1984). In this study forty-five children aged 4 to 6 years were interviewed about their understanding of written numerals in familiar contexts. The children came from a variety of backgrounds, but none of them had yet received formal instruction in reading, writing or arithmetic (children in Switzerland do not start school until the age of 6 years).

These children were shown a series of cards with pictures in which numbers were used in recognisable contexts. One picture, for example, showed a birthday cake with five candles, and a '5' in the middle; another showed a bus with the number '22' on it, while others showed numbers used on car licence-plates, on houses, and on shopping receipts. The children were interviewed informally about each picture and asked specific questions concerning the numeral, such as 'What is that?', 'What does it say?' and 'Why is that written there?'

The clearest finding to emerge from this study was the widespread recognition amongst the children that these numerals served a particular purpose – that they communicated information (usually but not always numerical) for the benefit of other people. Less than one-fifth of the children simply identified the numbers, while the great majority explicitly assigned some kind of function to every number. Some of these functions were very general: for example, the number on the bus was 'for the people who go on the bus', and the number on the licence-plate was 'for the policeman to look at'. Nearly half the children, however, were able to assign to the numeral a very specific function: for example, the cake with five candles was to show that 'he's five!' or that 'somebody was just five years old', while the number on the bus was to show 'which one it is', or 'if it's yours', or 'where it goes'. The Sinclairs were not too concerned with whether these specific functions were correct or not, and thus did not differentiate between the explanations that the number-plate showed 'how much the car cost' and that it showed 'whose car it is'. They pointed out that if one questions adults about pencilled numerals written on eggs (as they apparently did) then one obtains several different plausible interpretations, such as that they indicate the weight of the egg, its grade, its size, the hen who laid it, the date on which it was laid and so on. Their interest was not so much in children's knowledge of particular conventions, but in their more general understanding that numbers are used to convey information.

The children did not find it equally easy to attach particular functions to the different cards. Not surprisingly, given the importance of birthdays in the lives of young children, the '5' on the cake produced the highest number of specific ascriptions. The second easiest card was the one showing numbered buttons in a lift – less surprising than it might seem, given the architectural character of Geneva. The Sinclairs point out that the pictures of the cake and the lift were the only ones showing numbers in proximity to the appropriate number of objects (candles and buttons), and argue that this may explain the ease of these two items. The hardest item was the car licence-plate, where the function of the numbers in everyday life is far from clear.

Children's understanding of arithmetical symbolism

This interesting study shows that, at least in Geneva, pre-school children are acquiring a good deal of information about environmental numerals before they start school. In contrast, children do not usually encounter operator signs such as ' + ', ' – ', or ' = ' until they start school, and their natural interaction with the environment does not even bring them to their attention. Instead, they learn about these signs in the much more artificial context of the classroom.

The findings reported in chapter 5 revealed a striking reluctance amongst school-age children, when questioned outside the classroom, to use the signs ' + ', ' − ' and ' = ' to represent actions performed with bricks. These findings made me wonder how children would react if asked to carry out the *opposite* translation, from arithmetical symbolism back to concrete situations. Would they, for example, understand that '3 + 4 = 7' could be represented by the action of adding together a group of three bricks and a group of four bricks, resulting in a group of seven bricks? This question seemed to be the mirror-image of the one which Miranda Jones and I had asked earlier.

As far as I could tell, there had been no previous research on this particular topic, and I therefore had to start from scratch. I decided to write some arithmetical symbols on cards, and to ask school-age children to demonstrate the meaning of these symbols by using bricks. The choice of symbols was also intended to mirror our previous work: thus one card simply carried the numeral '5', two cards showed numerals and operator signs (' +3' and ' −2') and two cards showed complete operations ('3 + 4 = 7' and '6 − 2 = 4'), as shown in figure 7.1.

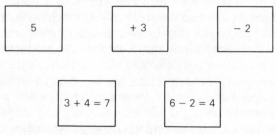

Figure 7.1   Set of five cards used in pilot work

I tried out these cards with a group of eleven children from a local middle-class primary school. The children were aged 5 to 7 years, and had been chosen by their teachers as representing the full spectrum of mathematical ability in the school. All the children were using arithmetical symbols in their school work.

I used various questions to try to elicit from the children what they thought the numbers and signs on the card meant. Typically, I would put the cards face-down in a small stack on the table, next to a pile of bricks, and say, 'Now I'm going to turn over each card. I want you to show me what's on the card, show me what it means, using the bricks.' I then turned over one card at a time and asked 'Can you show me what that means?' After that my questioning tried, as far as possible, to follow and elucidate the children's thinking.

I had very few preconceptions of how the children would react to these problems. It seemed to me quite possible that they would find them trivially easy. Similarly, I had only some vague notions of what a 'correct' answer would be. I imagined that they might represent the '5' by constructing a group of five bricks, that they might represent ' +3' by adding three bricks to a pile, and that they might represent '3 + 4 = 7' by pushing together a group of three bricks and a group of four bricks. However, I did not want to rule out other responses: I just wanted to see what the children would make of the task.

The children in fact reacted very differently to the different cards. The '5' caused little difficulty: all but one of the children simply counted out five bricks from the pile and showed me in some way that this group of five bricks represented what was on the card. Some children built a tower out of the five bricks whereas others just put them in a rough heap. Two children organised them into a neat cross.

One child, however, responded in a quite unexpected way. This was Jamie, aged 6 years. When first shown the card he asked, 'Do I make a five?': I assumed he meant should he put out five bricks, and so I said that this would be fine. He started moving the bricks hesitantly and did not seem to have a clear idea of what he was doing. I said: 'Show me what's on the card, using the bricks. That's the thing to do. Show me what it means.' Jamie then started arranging the bricks very carefully in the shape of a number 5 (figure 7.2).

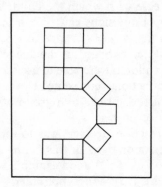

Figure 7.2 Jamie's representation of '5'

MH: Oh, I see what you're trying to do, you're trying to make a thing like that with the bricks (tracing with finger round the '5' on the card). Is that what you're trying to do?

Jamie: Yes, but it's a bit square.

MH: It wasn't really what I meant. What I really meant was I want you to pretend that I don't know anything about numbers and things, and you've got to show me what they mean. Okay? So if I put that card down and say I don't know what that means, can you use the bricks to show me what it means? Can you do that? (Jamie wriggles uncertainly.) Pretend I was a little boy and you were having to explain it to me. Could you do that?

Jamie: Well I think so. (But he doesn't do anything.)

MH: (Puts the bricks back into the pile.) Are you going to have another go at that, trying to explain what that means to me?

Jamie: It's a number.

MH: Yes.

Jamie: And it's after four.

MH: Yes, I see. Could you use these bricks to show me what it is?

Jamie: You mean make a picture of it again?

MH: Is that the only way you can think of doing it? (Jamie nods.)

I was surprised to find a child who interpreted the question in the way that Jamie did. I was equally surprised by the difficulty which Jamie had in grasping the idea that there might be a *different* way of using the bricks to explain the meaning of '5'. Jamie was the only child who responded to the '5' in this way, although, as we shall see, there were several children who, for some of the other cards, focused on the superficial appearance of the symbols rather than considering their meaning.

In contrast to the ease with which the children represented the '5', the cards showing operator signs caused considerable difficulty. The complete operations ('3 + 4 = 7' and '6 − 2 = 4') were instantly recognised by the children as being the familiar sums of their classroom. However, only three children were able to use the bricks to demonstrate the additions and subtractions represented by these sums – for example, by adding a group of four bricks to a group of three, and indicating that there were now seven bricks.

A more frequent reaction, in fact, was to represent the superficial appearance of the operator signs in this 'sum' in a similar fashion to Jamie's representation of '5'. A good example is provided by Rachel, a 6-year-old (see figure 7.3). When presented with the card showing '3 + 4 = 7', she said musingly, 'Three and four is seven,' and thought for a while. Then, proceeding from left to right, she put out a group of three bricks, then a single brick ('That's to make the "and" sign'), then a group of four bricks, and then two rows of two bricks ('That's to make the "makes"'). At this point, she discovered that she was left with only one brick. She put this to the right of her 'makes' sign. 'Not enough bricks. We haven't got seven. That'll have to make up for seven.'

Rachel's attempt to represent the whole sum was thus thwarted by my lack of foresight – I had not provided a sufficient number of bricks, for it had never occurred to me that any of the children would respond in this way!

A similar response was produced by Keene, a 7-year-old, when presented with the subtraction problem '6 – 2 = 4'. He said, 'That's easy', and put out groups of six, two and four bricks. He added a single brick between the groups of six and two to represent the ' – ', and would have added a further brick to represent the ' = ' but again he had run out of bricks (see figure 7.3).

The shortage of bricks also presented a problem for Jamie, as one might have predicted. This was perhaps fortunate, as his efforts were very pains-taking and time-consuming; he did not get very far with the first complete sum (see figure 7.3), and I decided not to ask him to represent the second.

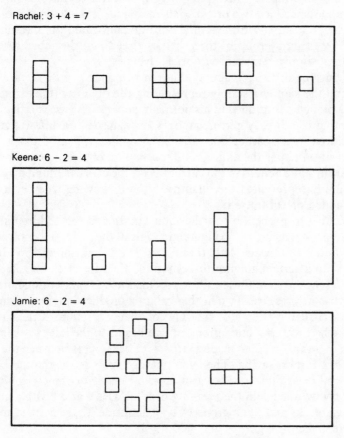

Rachel: 3 + 4 = 7

Keene: 6 – 2 = 4

Jamie: 6 – 2 = 4

Figure 7.3   Representations of addition and subtraction

The cards which caused the most difficulty were those which simply showed a numeral and an operator sign, ' + 3' and ' – 2'. This is perhaps not surprising, given that these 'incomplete' combinations of symbols were unfamiliar to the children: in their normal classroom work they had only come across complete sums. Nevertheless, I had thought that at least some of the children might interpret these combinations as representing part of an addition or subtraction. That is, they might have represented ' + 3' by adding three bricks to the rest of the pile, as in the Pile task of chapter 5, and ' – 2' by taking away two bricks from the pile.

There were only four occasions when children seemed to grasp the idea that ' + 3', or ' – 2' could be interpreted as a dynamic event. Della, a 7-year-old, counted out six bricks for ' + 3' and explained that she thought I had meant 'three plus three'. Claire, a 6-year-old, put out three and then added two bricks to them saying, 'If I add on two bricks it's five.' Rachel and Emily-Anne both demonstrated the meaning of ' – 2' by using a group of three bricks already on the table: in each case they simply removed two bricks from it.

All but one of the remaining children responded to these cards by ignoring the sign and simply representing the quantity (the exception was Jamie, who continued in his normal manner). This was particularly interesting as it directly mirrored the responses made by a different group of children to the earlier Pile task. These children had been asked to represent on paper the addition or subtraction of a number of bricks to or from a pile and, as in the current task, the overwhelming majority had simply represented the quantity without showing whether it had been added or subtracted.

I decided to probe a bit further and questioned the children about the ' + ' or '-' which they had ignored. Some of the children simply said, 'It's "and"', 'It means "add three"' or 'It's a "take-away"'. Others, often with a certain amount of hesitation, placed a brick on the table to represent the sign: these children seemed to be representing nothing more than its presence. Two further children produced responses similar to those elicited by the cards showing complete operations. One of these was Rachel, who put out a group of five bricks to the left of her initial group of three. She then made a cross with her fingers between the two groups of bricks, saying 'Then you put an "and" in the middle.' The other child was Steven, a 7-year-old, who became extremely confused when trying to explain the meaning of ' – 2'. He started with a group of three bricks and put a group of two alongside it. He pointed to the space between the groups and said:

Well...you could...Three take away two leaves one if you go like that (puts the two bricks on top of the group of three bricks, then takes them off again)...coz...if you have three (takes one more from pile, adds it to his group of two bricks: he now has two groups of three) take away two (points to the space between the two groups and then to the right-hand group of three)...leaves one...(removes one from his right-hand group of three)...well ...that's better (and pushes the remaining two bricks of the right-hand group back into the pile; pushes the remaining group of three into the middle of the table). Three take away two leaves one (pushes two bricks away from this group) and if you were doing a sum (puts the two bricks back with the single brick) like that (gets two more bricks to make a second group on the right) you'd put the 'take-away' there (points to the space between the groups) and put the answer there (points to the space to the right of the right-hand group).

I had not expected that these simple tasks would cause such problems. Nor had I expected them to reveal such a striking range of understanding in the children. The impression which I got from several of the children was that the signs ' + ', ' − ' and ' = ' had little immediate relevance to the world of ordinary objects, but inhabited the self-contained world of 'sums'. It seemed to be difficult for many of the children to conceive of the signs' existence outside this world.

There is, of course, a danger of drawing too many conclusions from such a limited sample. There was a clear need to repeat this study with a larger group of children. It was also important to find out whether the children would produce the same kind of responses if the rationale for the task was made clearer. Finally, it seemed important to explore the relationship between the children's responses and their wider mathematical ability: could it be that those few children who were able to produce adequate representations of sums such as '3 + 4 = 7' and '6 − 2 = 4' also did particularly well in their mathematics work in school, while the children who produced superficial representations of these sums had considerable difficulty with school mathematics, and understood it only superficially?

Children's explanations of arithmetical symbolism

These questions provided the focus of a much larger study carried out by Anna Stallard (1982). She used sixty children aged 6 years 3 months to 10 years 6 months, from a middle-class school in Edinburgh. The children were chosen at random from five separate classes, but their teachers were afterwards asked to rate each child as 'good', 'average', or 'poor' at mathematics.

Anna Stallard improved on my procedure by presenting the children with a much clearer rationale for explaining the meaning of the symbols. She used the large toy panda called Chu-Chu (mentioned briefly in chapter 5) who had featured in several earlier experiments carried out by Margaret Donaldson. These experiments had shown that young children often gave explanations to the panda which they would not do to an adult. This was particularly likely to happen if it was put to the children that the panda did not understand things and needed their help: children seem to be more expressive and articulate in a role whereby they imagine that they are helping someone smaller and less knowledgeable than themselves.

Anna Stallard introduced Chu-Chu to the children and asked them to pretend that the panda did not understand what was written on the cards. She said, 'I want you to try and show the panda what the cards mean, so that he will understand them, using these bricks to help you, okay?' After they had attempted to explain a particular card to the panda, they were asked whether or not the panda could understand the card now, and were generally encouraged to think about whether or not their response conveyed the meaning of the card. The adequacy of each response was subsequently assessed, the crucial factor being that the meaning and not just the appearance of the card had to have been conveyed. This could be done either by using the bricks, as suggested, or by a purely verbal explanation.

The children were shown a much wider range of cards than I had used in my pilot work. For example, one of the cards just showed the zero sign ('0'), while two cards included zero as part of complete addition and subtraction sums ('5 − 5 = 0' and '4 + 0 = 4'). Stallard also used a number of cards which showed numerals and operator signs being used in an unusual and unfamiliar form: two showed a single numeral and operator sign ('− 5' and '+ 6'), similar to those I had used earlier; two showed complete addition and subtraction sums, but presented in a 'reversed' form ('7 = 5 + 2' and '4 = 6 − 2'); and one card showed the equality '3 = 3'. The complete set of cards used is shown in figure 7.4.

Anna Stallard found, as I had, that some cards were much easier to explain than others. As before, the cards bearing just the numerals '6' and '2' were the easiest, with most children simply showing the appropriate number of bricks. There were, however, a few examples of children who, like Jamie, produced pictorial representations of the

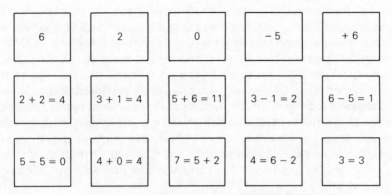

Figure 7.4   Set of fifteen cards used by Anna Stallard (1982).

numerals. In contrast, cards showing both numerals and operator signs were much harder to explain (see table 7.1).

TABLE 7.1   Adequacy score (%) for each card (from Stallard, 1982)

Card	Score (%)
6	95
2	93
0	85
5 − 5 = 0	62
2 + 2 = 4	62
3 − 1 = 2	60
1 + 3 = 4	58
6 − 5 = 1	57
5 + 6 = 11	55
4 = 6 − 2	47
7 = 5 + 2	45
− 5	43
+ 6	35
4 + 0 = 4	30
3 = 3	18

Of the cards showing operator signs as well as numerals, those showing conventional 'sums' were the easiest, with between half and two-thirds of the children producing adequate representations. Most of these involved the dynamic movement of groups of bricks to demonstrate the additions and subtractions. Some of the children, however, gave inventive verbal descriptions. There was one 9-year-old girl who, for '3 − 1 = 2', explained: 'There are three buses at the bus stop and you get on one and it goes away and there are two left.' For '1 + 3 = 4' she said: 'You go to the shop and buy an apple and your mum says, "Your dad and me and Tracy want one too", so you go back and buy three more and you've got four.' As before, some children produced static demonstrations of the superficial appearance of the sum, as in figure 7.3. There were also some responses which mixed a static display with a verbal description. For example, one child laid out groups of one, three and four bricks and said 'Take one brick and three more bricks, count them up and you've got four': this child was credited with an 'adequate' explanation.

The cards bearing or including zero produced an interesting range of responses. The card showing zero on its own was adequately represented by well over three-quarters of the children. Their responses were mostly verbal, such as 'None there', 'Put no bricks in front', 'Haven't got any bricks at all', in each case accompanied by either the removal of all the bricks from the table, or a refusal to add any bricks to the empty space in front of them. Some children, on the other hand, used the bricks to make pictorial representations of zero (see figure 7.5).

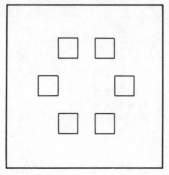

Figure 7.5   Representation of zero
(from Stallard, 1982, p. 27)

The two addition and subtraction problems involving zero differed quite strikingly in the adequacy of the responses which they elicited. The card with '5 − 5 = 0' caused no particular difficulties due to the presence of the zero, and this sum was adequately represented by two-thirds of the children. In contrast, '4 + 0 = 4' was adequately represented by less than a third of the children, with the presence of zero in the second position causing particular difficulties. A number of children simply placed four bricks on the table and said nothing. Other children did this but at the same time made various verbal attempts to convey the meaning of the sum. Thus one child put four bricks on the table and said, 'Add nothing'; she then moved the group over to the right-hand side of the table, said 'Makes four', and moved the group back. Another child put four bricks on the table, took them off to show zero, and finally placed them back again.

The cards which showed a numeral and an operator sign ('– 5' and '+ 6') were more difficult than those showing a complete sum. Some of the children suggested that these cards were in some sense not fair: 'We don't do them kind of sums', or 'We haven't done those yet'. Another child said, 'You wouldn't show the sign as it's not got a number at the start.' As before, the most common response was simply to count out the number of bricks represented by the numeral and ignore the operator sign. Curiously enough, this type of response was produced over three times as often to the '+ 6' card as to the '– 5' card.

Other children made more successful attempts to convey what was going on. One child responded to the '+ 6' card by saying, 'There'd be nothing there and then put six', while several children converted these messages into a complete sum which they could represent. This response was judged to be adequate if the child gave a full explanation which retained the meaning of what was on the card. The card showing '– 5' was usually converted into the sum '5 – 5 = 0'. One child, however, said 'Nothing take away five leaves...' and started to produce a static display of this sum (figure 7.6). Leaving an empty space at the left-hand side of the table, he positioned four bricks in a row to make the '–'; he added a group of five to the right of that, and then positioned six bricks (in two rows) for the '='. At this point he refused to continue, saying: 'You can't do that. You've got to have a bigger number on that side to take away from that side.'

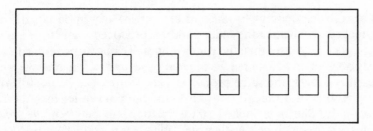

Figure 7.6   Representation of 'nothing take away five'
(from Stallard, 1982, p. 46)

The 'reversed' sums also produced comments of dismay from the children: 'Wrong way round' was typical, or 'Doesn't make sense'. A frequent response was simply to turn the sums round and represent the more familiar form. If meaning was preserved, and the new explanation adequate, then this response was scored as adequate. One child, for '4 = 6 – 2', gave a verbal explanation: 'Six sweeties and you give your friend a sweetie and have one yourself and you've got four left.'

Finally, the card showing the equality '3 = 3' drew puzzled looks from many of the children, and was by far the most difficult for them to represent. Nearly three-quarters of the children produced a simple static array, showing three bricks, six bricks, or some sort of equation (see figure 7.7), but this was rarely accompanied by an adequate verbal explanation.

It was hardly surprising that this last card should prove so difficult. It is indeed hard even for an adult to think of an adequate way of explaining its meaning. Nevertheless, most adults would accept that it was a legitimate statement, albeit a rather strange one. In contrast, most of the children clearly thought that there was 'something wrong' or 'something missing' with this particular juxtaposition of symbols.

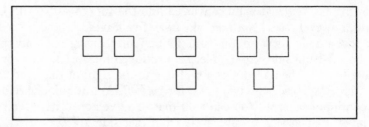

Figure 7.7   Representation of '3 = 3'
(from Stallard, 1982, p. 47)

Two further findings by Stallard are particularly important. First, she looked at whether the older children produced a greater number of adequate responses than the younger ones. To our surprise, she found *no relationship at all between the children's ages and their adequacy scores:* at each age-level, the same proportion of children had difficulty with the questions, and the 10-year-olds found them no easier than did the 6-year-olds. She then looked at the relationship between children's adequacy scores and their mathematics ability (as rated by their teachers). Here she found that *those children rated as 'good' at mathematics performed significantly better – at all ages – than those rated 'average' or 'poor'.*

These are two unexpected and very important findings. It is not clear how much the teachers' ratings reflect the children's all-round general ability, or whether a specific mathematical ability is involved: further research would be needed to answer that question. Nevertheless, whatever the ability involved, it seems to be relatively independent of the stage the children had reached in the mathematics curriculum. Children in the youngest class who were 'good' outperformed those in the highest class who were 'average' or 'poor', even though most of the older children would be some way ahead of the younger children in their school mathematics work.

The effect of 'doing sums' on children's understanding of symbols

Anna Stallard's findings make a sharp and poignant contrast to those of Anne and Hermine Sinclair, described earlier in this chapter. The Sinclair study shows that pre-school children learn about the numerals '1', '2', '3', etc., through their normal everyday activities. Even before they start school, children are aware that numerals are used in a variety of situations and for a variety of purposes, some of which are to do with representing quantity and some not. In contrast, children come across the operator signs ' + ', ' − ' and ' = ' in only one context, that of the classroom. Moreover, they come to associate these symbols with one very specific classroom activity, namely 'doing sums'.

What associations are the children likely to make? Normally, sums are laid out as follows:

$$3 + 4 = \quad \text{or} \quad 6 - 2 =$$

The empty space or box to the right of the ' = ' tells the child that their task is to complete the equation. Thus, they will come to learn that ' = ' means 'do something to the left-hand side and put the answer on the right-hand side.' What is to be done depends on what is on the left-hand side. If there is a ' + ' then the problem is an 'add', and the two numbers must be added together. If there is a ' − ' then it is a 'take-away', and one number (usually the smaller) must be subtracted from the other. The child will thus come to acquire some very specific meanings for the operator signs ' + ', ' − ' and ' = ': these signs will not easily be seen as representations of events or relationships involving concrete objects, but will instead be experienced by the child as stimuli to 'do something' to the surrounding numbers.

Anna Stallard's findings suggest that these limited meanings of ' + ', ' – ' and ' = ' are widely held by British school children. They were also found to be widespread in a group of American children studied by Merlyn Behr, Stanley Erlwanger and Eugene Nichols in 1980. This study, entitled 'How Children View the Equals Sign', was prompted by the question of whether children consider 'equals' to be an operator or a relation. As an operator, ' = ' would be a 'do something' signal along the lines indicated above. As a relational symbol, ' = ' would indicate an equivalence between what is written before and after it.

Behr and his colleagues presented children aged 6 to 12 years with various written and spoken 'addition sentences' (including the forms '2 + 4 = ', '☐ = 4 + 5' and '2 + 3 = 3 + 2'), and asked them to explain what these 'sentences' meant. The findings were in very close agreement with Anna Stallard's. For example, the children clearly thought that '2 + 4 ' was a stimulus for an answer which needed to be placed on the right. They tended to reject the form of sentences like '☐ = 4 + 5' and change it to '4 + 5 = ☐', or '☐ + 4 = 5'. One 6-year-old, for example, explained that such a sentence was 'backwards' and asked the interviewer, 'Do you read backwards?' The children also showed a strong tendency to reject statements like '3 + 2 = 2 + 3'. For example, one 7-year-old said of it: 'You need to change it to "plus"', and rewrote it as '3 + 2 + 2 + 3 = 10'. Behr and his colleagues concluded as follows:

> These interviews suggest that children consider the symbol = as a 'do something signal'. There is a strong tendency among all of the children to view the = symbol as being acceptable in a sentence only when one (or more) operation signs (+, –, etc.) precede it. Some children, in fact, tell us that the answer must come after the equal sign. We observe in the children's behaviour an extreme rigidity about written sentences, an insistence that statements be written in a particular form, and a tendency to perform actions (e.g., add) rather than to reflect, make judgments, and infer meanings.

It is clear that young children's understanding of ' = ' is very different from that of its inventor, Robert Recorde, when he justified its form by saying that 'noe 2. thynges, can be moare equalle' than a pair of parallel lines of equal length. But this limited understanding is not simply restricted to young children. Josette Adda (1982) quotes an unpublished study by W. M. Brookes, in which adults were asked to look at '7 + 8 = 14' and correct the mistake. Brookes found that the overwhelming reaction to this question was to replace the '14' with '15': it was much rarer to replace the '8' with '7', or the '7' with '6'. Adda concludes (p. 206): 'This shows that the asymmetric meaning of " = " is pregnant for all of us.'

It might be argued that such a view of the equals sign is not by itself too damaging. It might even be argued that this understanding is actually helpful when using calculators. For example, if a calculator is to be used for the addition '3 + 4', then the child must press the keys in the order: '3', ' + ', '4' and ' = '. In this situation, pressing the ' = ' key is appropriately seen as instructing the calculator to work out the total.

Clearly, there are times when it useful to understand operator signs as instructions. The point is not that this understanding of them is incorrect, but that it should not preclude other ways of understanding them. For example, when children move on to learn algebra, it is essential that they grasp the idea of the equals sign as showing an equivalence between the two sides of an equation. If a child believes that there is something 'wrong' with '3 + 2 = 2 + 3', and wants to change the ' = ' to a ' + ', then what hope has this child of responding correctly to the equation '$3x + 2 = 2x + 3$'? Algebra uses the equivalence of such relationships as the basis for calculating the value of 'x'.

Overview

The studies described in this chapter have exposed serious limitations in children's understanding of arithmetical symbols. Most children learn about these symbols through 'doing sums', and only seem sure of themselves when confronted with standard equations in a familiar form. Even then, many children find it difficult to express the underlying meaning of these equations: their understanding of written symbolism appears to be extremely superficial. Only rarely does one find children like the girl on p. 106 who can readily translate from this symbolism into everyday situations.

These findings provide a very clear parallel to the findings described in chapter 5. There is now substantial evidence that children have severe problems when asked to translate between different representations of arithmetical concepts – either from concrete to written (chapter 5) or from written to concrete (chapter 7). There is also evidence from Anna Stallard's study that children's reluctance to translate between the written and the concrete is directly related to their performance in school mathematics, regardless of the stage they have reached in the curriculum. This suggests that translation problems not only occur in the tasks which we devised, but may also play an important part in the difficulties which many children experience when learning mathematics in school. We will examine this possibility more closely in the next chapter.

8

Children's difficulties in school

In this chapter we will look more closely at ways in which translation problems might be involved in children's difficulties with school arithmetic. First we will look at some 8-year-old children working at column subtraction problems, and see if they are helped by using concrete materials when they are stuck. Later we will look at some younger children (aged 5 to 6 years) to see whether they also make use of an opportunity to translate between concrete and written versions of problems which are causing them difficulty. For each group of children we will see how their understanding of school arithmetic is severely limited by their reluctance – or inability – to translate between the different types of representation.

Children's difficulties with column subtraction problems

One area in which children frequently encounter difficulties is when they are learning how to perform column subtraction problems like the following:

$$97 \qquad\qquad 93$$
$$-43 \qquad\qquad -47$$

The problem on the left is relatively easy, and most children quickly learn that this can be solved by performing the two much simpler subtractions, '7 – 3' and '9 – 4'. The problem on the right is much more difficult. As children frequently point out, 'you can't take 7 from 3', and so a new method must be learnt.

Problems like this can in fact be solved by more than one method. The traditional method is generally known in Britain as 'borrow and pay back', although it is more accurately described as 'equal addition'. In this method, the problem is solved by adding ten to both numbers. The '10' which is added to the number on the upper line appears in the form of a small '1' to the left of the '3'. This in effect converts it into 'ninety-thirteen', and the '7' can now be subtracted from '13'. Children using this method are taught that as '10 has been borrowed', it must also be 'paid back'. This is done by placing another small '1' next to the '4' in the lower line, to show that the lower number should now be read as '57'. The problem is completed by subtracting 5 from 9 (see below).

$$
\begin{array}{r}
{}^{1} \\
93 \\
-\,{}_{1}47 \\
\hline
46
\end{array}
$$

The second main method, currently more popular in Britain, is known as 'decomposition'. With this method the number in the top line, '93', is decomposed into '80' and '13': as before, a small '1' is placed next to the '3', but this time it is compensated for by converting the '9' into '8'. The problem is now solved by subtracting '7' from '13', and '4' from '8' (see below).

$$
\begin{array}{r}
8\ | \\
\not{9}3 \\
-47 \\
\hline
46
\end{array}
$$

There are advantages and disadvantages to both these methods. Advocates of 'borrow and pay back' claim that it is relatively straightforward to teach and to learn, and they also point out the difficulties of working out by decomposition a problem such as:

$$
\begin{array}{r}
10003 \\
-\quad\ 6 \\
\hline
\end{array}
$$

Advocates of decomposition argue that the above calculation is difficult whatever method is used, and that their method is inherently more comprehensible to children, as it corresponds to how the subtraction would be carried out using concrete materials. In the '93 – 47' problem, for example, decomposition can be understood as exchanging a concrete representation of '10' for ten concrete 'units'. In practice, children do not appear to find either method particularly easy. This is no doubt because both methods require a good understanding of the difficult concept of place-value.

Children's difficulties with column subtraction problems have been studied intensively in recent years. Particularly interesting is the line of research started by John Seely Brown and Richard Burton (1978), and continued by, amongst others, Kurt VanLehn (1983). In this research, children's performance on subtraction problems is analysed in terms of their faulty procedures or 'bugs'. Bugs are different from errors or slips in that they *systematically* reveal themselves in a number of different situations. For example, one of the most common subtraction bugs is known as 'smaller-from-larger'. A child whose method is bugged in this way will always subtract a smaller number from a larger number, instead of 'borrowing' or using the method of decomposition. Such a child, when faced with the pair of problems illustrated earlier, will give the same answer, '54', to both problems.

My own interest in column subtraction problems arose from a slightly different point of view. I wanted to know whether there was any relationship between children's difficulties with these problems and their ability to translate between concrete and written representations. In particular I wanted to know whether children who were having difficulties with a column subtraction problem would consider it *useful* to translate the problem into a corresponding concrete representation. This presupposed that they were in fact *able* to make such a translation, and I was beginning to doubt whether this assumption could be made.

I obtained some initial answers to these questions when observing a mathematics class in an Edinburgh school. The school served a predominantly middle-class area. The children were around 8 years old and were learning to do subtractions involving three-digit numbers by the method of decomposition. For some of the problems it was necessary to use the method of decomposition twice, and their teacher referred to this as 'double-decomposition'.

For most of the lesson the children were working on written problems which involved varying degrees of decomposition. Available on their tables were boxes of concrete materials, versions of the Dienes Multi-base Arithmetic Blocks commonly used in primary mathematics classrooms. They consisted of wooden pieces of different sizes. The smallest were little wooden cubes with sides about a centimetre long. Then there were long thin strips, equivalent to ten small cubes placed in a row. The largest were flat squares, equivalent to ten strips placed side by side. The children referred to them as 'ones', 'tens' and 'hundreds'. According to their teacher, they had had plenty of experience with these materials, and knew how to use them to carry out the subtraction problems in their work-books.

It was quite clear after only a few moments of observation that the children were generally reluctant to use the materials when working on written problems. They preferred to stick with paper and pencil even when they were clearly having difficulty. The only children I could see who spontaneously used the materials were those identified by their teacher as belonging to the lowest mathematics group. I decided to observe individual children more closely to look at how they attempted these problems.

Michael

The first child I observed was Michael. He was in the top mathematics group and approached problems in his work-book confidently. I watched him carry out a number of problems involving double-decomposition, and he was successful each time. He completed a set of exercises and took them out to his teacher to be marked. He came back and showed me that all but one of his answers had received a tick. The exception was this one:

$$\begin{array}{r} \overset{2}{2}\overset{1}{\cancel{3}}4 \\ -108 \\ \hline 126 \end{array}$$

This was very interesting. Michael's teacher had accidentally marked his correct answer wrong – a rare lapse for her. Michael, however, did not seem perturbed by this. He took out his rubber, quickly erased the '2' from his answer, and replaced it with a '0' as shown below:

$$\begin{array}{r} \overset{2}{2}\overset{1}{\cancel{3}}4 \\ -108 \\ \hline 106 \end{array}$$

I asked him why he'd done that. 'Well,' he said, 'I took nought from two, and got two, when it should have been nought.'

This was even more interesting. Here was Michael, an apparently competent child, replacing his correct answer with an incorrect one, and justifying it with an explanation which a moment's thought would undermine. I asked him if he was sure he was right. He paused, then reworked his sum. This time he got the same answer as before, namely '126'. Yet this had been marked wrong. For the first time he looked puzzled.

I suggested he use the materials to work it out, and he agreed that this might help. To my surprise, he started by laying out the concrete equivalence not of the initial quantity, '234', but of his *answer*, '126'. He looked at the arrangement for a while, then exchanged a 'ten' for ten 'ones'. He justified this with the comment: 'Coz you can't do it.' He then laid out materials representing '108' underneath his first set, as in figure 8.1. He now announced his intention of subtracting the second set from the first, but soon had got quite lost. At this point he was rescued by his teacher who called him to the front of the classroom to discuss some other work he had done. 'I've got to go,' he said with some relief, rapidly gathering all the materials together and replacing them in the box.

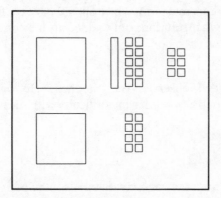

Figure 8.1 Michael's representation of '234–108'

This brief episode with Michael revealed two very interesting features. First there was the way he 'repaired' his sum – to use the terminology developed by VanLehn (1983) – by changing his correct subtraction, '2 – 0 = 2', to the incorrect one, '2 – 0 = 0'. Clearly he was not thinking very deeply about what he was doing, but was simply looking for the most likely source of error. Presumably his previous experience had led him to the conclusion that this would involve zero.

Michael's assumption here is in fact supported by other research on children's subtraction errors, which shows that zero is indeed a common source of error. An explanation for this has been reported by James Brannin (1982). He states (p. 7) that all his subjects who made errors involving zero 'explained their solutions by stating that zero signifies "nothing", and hence the arithmetic operations customarily applied to other numbers cannot be used when dealing with it.' This certainly ties in with my own observations on children's understanding of zero. As we have seen, even pre-school children deal easily with the idea of a symbol to represent 'none' in the context of the Tins game (see chapter 5). Their difficulties seem to start when they encounter zero in the context of a sum, as Anna Stallard's study clearly shows (see chapter 7).

The second interesting feature of Michael's performance was the totally unexpected difficulty he had in translating the written problem into concrete form. It was possible that the experience of having a problem marked wrong had seriously undermined his confidence. It was also possible that he had represented the answer, '126', simply because that was the number uppermost in his mind. He may even have been trying to work backwards from his answer to the original starting point of '234', but got lost on the way. Whatever the reason, the strategy of translating from written to concrete form, which should have confirmed the correctness of his original solution, only added to his confusion.

Stephen

The next child I observed was Stephen. He was in the middle mathematics group and was having difficulty with the following problem:

$$
\begin{array}{r}
2\ 3\ 4 \\
-\ \ 1\ 9 \\
\hline
\end{array}
$$

I suggested he used the concrete materials to help him, and he laid out the elements in his sum as in figure 8.2. He looked at the blocks and said, 'You can't take nine from four, so I think you substitute.' When asked what he meant, he replied, 'You can't take nine from four, so you have to go next door and take away four.' Apparently the metaphor of 'going next door' was one that his teacher had used in explaining the procedure for double-decomposition. I asked him again what he meant. 'You can't do nine from four, you've got to go next door and borrow. So three becomes two.'

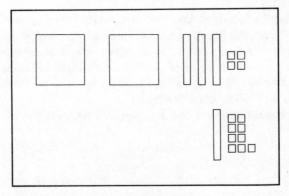

Figure 8.2   Stephen's representation of '234 – 19'

Stephen moved a 'ten' from the left-hand side of the 'ones' to the right-hand side. Then he got ten 'ones' from the box, and added them to the four. He stared at this arrangement for some time, but seemed unable to go any further. Eventually he returned to his work-book and carried out the subtraction correctly. He did not appear to be using double-decomposition, and may in fact have 'built up' his answer in the way used by Tony in chapter 1 (see pp. 5–6). Stephen then laid out materials showing the correct answer and put all the rest back in the box!

Stephen did not show Michael's confusion in putting out his answer first. Nevertheless, he was strongly influenced by the superficial structure of the problem, and attempted to match this by laying out *both* the initial quantities. He then carried out a concrete analogue of the decomposition, but was still unable to 'subtract' one quantity from another. He *could* have done this by removing equal amounts from the two quantities until he was left with the answer, but this strategy did not occur to him. As with Michael, translating from written to concrete did not help him out of his difficulties.

Angela

The third child I observed was a girl called Angela, who was also in the middle mathematics group. She appeared to have mastered the method of double-decomposition and was using it successfully. I suggested she did a problem using the concrete materials. The next one was:

$$\begin{array}{r} 1\ 0\ 6 \\ -\ \ 3\ 2 \\ \hline \end{array}$$

Angela placed a 'hundred' and six 'ones' on the table. Next, she removed two 'ones' from the group of six. So far so good. However, at this point she failed to carry out a concrete analogue of the decomposition process. Instead she got out three 'tens', and put the 'hundred' back in the box. She added up the three 'tens' and four 'ones' with which she was left, and wrote in '34' as her answer.

The next problem was the one Stephen had attempted earlier:

$$234 - 19$$

Again, I suggested she used the concrete materials to carry out the calculation. She started by laying out two 'hundreds', three 'tens' and four 'ones'. She then removed the four 'ones' and replaced them with a 'ten'. She now had two 'hundreds' and four 'tens' on the table. She stared at this arrangement for a while, and then pushed the material away from her. She returned to her work-book and successfully completed the problem using double-decomposition.

Unlike Michael and Stephen, Angela did not attempt to represent more than one element in the problem. Nevertheless, having laid out the first quantity, she was unable to proceed. There seemed to be no connection in her mind between the method of decomposition which she was using and the notion of exchanging a concrete 'ten' for ten concrete units. As with the boys, translating into concrete materials seemed a fairly meaningless procedure.

It was quite striking that all three of the children whom I had observed found it so difficult to translate their written problems into concrete form. Translating in this way seemed to be an excellent strategy for helping them to understand and to use the complicated written procedure which they were learning. Indeed, the possibility of this concrete analogue is said to be the most important advantage of the decomposition method. In fact, the children observed here seemed to be only dimly aware that they were dealing with two different representations of the same problem, and that the two answers should therefore agree. Rather they seemed to regard the written procedure of decomposition and the concrete manipulation of materials as being two fundamentally unrelated activities.

Similar difficulties for American children

These observations must clearly be treated with caution, as they involve only a very small group of children in a single Scottish school. There is, however, some evidence that other children behave in ways which are very similar to the children described above.

In his book *Children's Arithmetic* (1977), Herbert Ginsburg gives many examples from his research with American children of the same kind of gap between children's understanding of written arithmetic and their understanding of more concrete situations. One example described by Ginsburg is a 9-year-old boy called George, who carried out the following subtraction:

$$
\begin{array}{r}
1\ 4 \\
-\ \ 5 \\
\hline
1\ 1 \\
\hline
\end{array}
$$

George's mistake is a nice example of the 'smaller-from-larger' bug mentioned earlier. He was given some paper-clips and asked to try again. The interviewer assumed that he would count out fourteen clips, remove five, and be left with nine. But, instead, George counted out five clips, then took away four to leave one. He then put out another clip, so that the two clips on the table resembled his answer: '11'. Instead of using the clips to represent the underlying meaning of the problem, he used them to represent the superficial appearance of his answer.

One of the most striking of Ginsburg's examples is from a 9-year-old called Patty. At one point Patty was asked to work out 'ten plus one'. She wrote down:

$$
\begin{array}{r}
1\ 0 \\
+\ 1 \\
\hline
2\ 0 \\
\hline
\end{array}
$$

Laying out problems in this way is a common mistake, and normally shows a lack of understanding of place-value. Patty's difficulties, however, seemed to run deeper than this. The interviewer asked her what she would do if she couldn't use paper. Patty replied that she would work it out on her fingers. She demonstrated by holding up all ten fingers and staring at them. The dialogue continued –

Patty: You have ten (she looked at her fingers). You put the zero on the bottom (draws a zero with her finger).
Interviewer: Just use your fingers now.
Patty: Then you put two and you add one and one and it's two.

The subsequent conversation revealed that Patty was incapable of using her fingers – and the interviewer's fingers, which were also offered to her – to work out the sum. Instead she attempted to reproduce on her fingers the physical appearance of her faulty sum. Despite the interviewer's probing, she failed to make the simple translation from paper to fingers.

Ginsburg's case-studies of American children are very similar to our own observations in Edinburgh. They show that for many children there is a serious split in their mathematical understanding between the concrete and the written. It is as if they inhabit two worlds, each with its own rules and procedures, but with little connection between the two.

What's the point of written symbolism?

In considering the origin of this split, it is easy to blame the children, and say that they are not thinking. It is also easy to blame the teachers, and say that they are being insensitive. But there is a further possibility, which is that young children do not see the *value* of using conventional written symbols. When they first come across these symbols, they do not help them to solve problems, and do not appear to have any obvious purpose. The symbols thus become associated with the artificial activity of 'doing sums', and are not seen as having anything to do with more ordinary situations.

It is worth looking more closely at the ways in which different types of written representation might help children solve problems. When they are first introduced to conventional written symbolism, children are usually capable of carrying out simple additions and subtractions involving small numbers of concrete objects. For example, they may know that adding two bricks to five bricks already in a box (as in the task described in chapter 3) will result in seven bricks in the box. Their difficulties are likely to start when slightly larger numbers are involved, such as when five bricks are added to nine bricks.

Symbolic

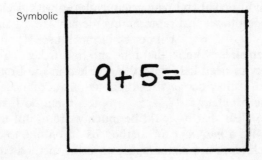

Pictographic

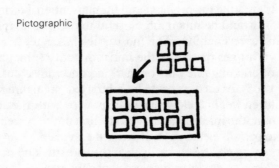

Iconic

Figure 8.3   Possible representations of addition problem

How might pencil and paper help children with such a problem? It is not difficult to see that representing the problem by the conventional symbolism '9 + 5 =   ' will not be of much use. If, on the one hand, the children already know that nine and five makes fourteen then they are unlikely to need help with the problem in the first place. On the other hand, if they do *not* already know this number fact, then representing the problem as '9 + 5 =   ' gets them no further forward.

It is also clear that it would be much more useful to represent the problem with a *non-standard* method based on one-to-one correspondence. If children use pictographic or iconic methods to represent the initial amount and the added amount (as in figure 8.3), then they will be left with the relatively simple task of working out the answer by counting the total number of bricks represented.

What about an equivalent subtraction problem, such as the removal of five bricks from a box containing nine? Again, children will not be helped by translating the problem into the conventional form '9 – 5 =   '. As before, it would be much more useful to use pictographic or iconic methods of representation. The most efficient strategy is probably to represent with lines or shapes the initial quantity (nine) and then use a method of crossing one out (or marking one with a dot, as Lindsay did in chapter 5) for each object to be subtracted (see figure 8.4). Alternatively, children might follow the strategy used with the addition, and represent both the initial amount and the amount to be removed. They now have to pair off elements to discover the 'remainder' or 'difference'.

What do young children actually do if they are stuck on such a problem and then given the opportunity to use paper and pencil? Do they attempt to represent the problem in conventional symbolism, even though this is not particularly helpful? Or do they devise some more useful method instead?

Written representations of hypothetical problems

Colin Brydon and I obtained some initial answers to these questions when we carried out some informal interviewing of 6-year-old children. These children attended the same middle-class school in which I carried out my earlier observations, and were at the beginning of their second year at school. They were familiar with conventional symbolism, and were using it to work on simple sums such as '5 + 2 = 7'. We saw the children in pairs to find out if they would benefit from discussing what to do. The problems we used were similar to the Hypothetical Shop questions used in chapter 3, and increased in difficulty until we

Symbolic

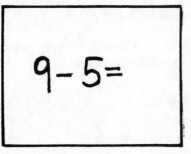

Pictographic

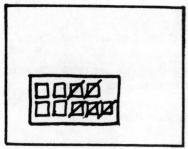
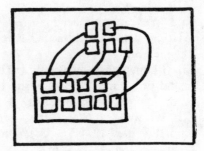

Iconic

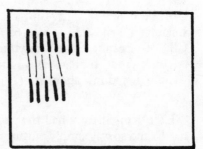

Figure 8.4 Possible representations of subtraction problem

reached a point at which the children either gave wrong answers or were unable to answer at all. We then provided them with paper and pencil, to see if this would help.

The first pair of children were two girls called Kim and Leanne. They managed very well until we reached the following point:

MH: Twelve children are going home on the school bus. Five children get off. How many are left on the bus?
Kim: Seven.
Leanne: Six.
MH: I wonder who's right. How did you work it out?
Kim: Thinked in my head.
MH: Thinking ahead? Oh, thinked in your head! What sort of thinking do you do?
Kim: You get the dots in your head.
MH: The dots?
Kim: Yes, in your head.
MH: So you Kim think it's seven, and you Leanne think it's...
Leanne: Six.
CB: I know what – we could try writing it down. (He produces paper and pens, and the girls write their names at the top.)
Kim: Do you do sums on it?
CB: We want you to do *this* sum. (Repeats the problem.)
Kim: (Writes '12 – 5 = 7') Seven.
Leanne: (Writes '12 – 6 =   '.)
CB: Leanne, how many children do you think got off the bus?
Leanne: Five.
MH: But what have you written down?
Kim: She's made a mistake.
CB: Are you going to write down that five got off?
Leanne: (Writes '12 – 5 =   '.)
CB: Yeah that's right, isn't it?
Leanne: (Writes '12 – 5 = 6'.)
CB: (To Leanne) Is there anything you can write down to help yourself think about it? (Pause.) Anything you can do on the paper, that will help you think about it? (No response.)

Here Kim already had the successful strategy of using 'dots in her head', and so was simply putting the answer down in conventional form. Leanne, however, did not appear to have such a strategy available: while she was able to represent the problem in conventional arithmetical symbolism, this did not help her to obtain the answer. But there was also her intriguing error: why should she write the problem down as '12 − 6 = '? Was it simply a mistake? Or was she actually on her way to writing down '12 − 6 = 6', a version which fitted in with her earlier answer of 'Six'?

The next problem was: 'Suppose there are fifteen icecreams in a freezer in a shop, and a lady in the shop sells eight of them. How many will be left?' This time Kim offered an incorrect answer, 'Ten', and Leanne repeated it after her. We indicated that this was wrong, and suggested that they used paper and pencil to work out the answer. As before, we saw the strange phenomenon of a child writing down a different problem from the one given. This time it was Kim who wrote: '15 − 5 = '. She corrected herself when it was pointed out. Now both girls were faced with the problem: '15 − 8 = '.

CB: Is there anything you could write down to help you work it out? (No response.) Could you draw anything? (No response.) Would it help if you drew some icecreams? (Kim and Leanne shake their heads.) Supposing you drew fifteen icecreams, and then drew eight of them being eaten, or put a cross through them, or something − pretend they got eaten − would that help you to find out how many were left?
Kim: I don't want to do that, I just want to think in my head.
MH: (To Leanne) Do you want to draw it, or think in your head?
Leanne: Think in my head.

There was a long silence while the girls thought in their heads, but no answer emerged. We could perhaps have suggested that Kim at least could try to represent on paper the 'dots in her head', but this did not occur to us. The problem was finally solved by using bricks. The girls counted out fifteen bricks, took away eight, and counted the remaining seven bricks. But by then the icecreams had long been forgotten.

This session confirmed our suspicion that writing problems down as conventional sums would not help them obtain a solution. But we had not expected that Kim and Leanne would reject so clearly the suggestion of drawing the icecreams to get the answer. Nor had we expected that they might write down slightly different sums which fitted more closely with the incorrect answers they had given.

The second pair of children were two boys called Ian and Kevin. The first problem on which they encountered difficulty was the following: 'There are twelve icecreams in a shop, and five get eaten. How many icecreams are left?'

Kevin: Ten.

Ian: Ten.

CB: Can you write down anything on the paper to help you work out if your answer's correct? (Kevin and Ian both write '10'.)

MH: Can you write anything else? There were twelve icecreams in the shop and five got eaten. How many are left? (Kevin and Ian both write '12' separately from the '10'.)

CB: Does that help you? (No response.)

The final pair were two boys called Mark and Jason. Their difficulties arose at a lower level than had those of the other children:

MH: There are eight boxes of chocolates in a shop, and three are sold. How many are left?

Mark: (Instantly) Three!

Jason: (Thinks for a bit.) Seven.

Mark: (Thinks for a bit.) Four?

CB: Would it help to write it down?

Jason, Mark: Mmmm. . .(but don't write anything).

The problem was repeated to them, but neither Jason nor Mark was able to write it down as a sum, or indeed to make any kind of representation of it.

These initial observations by Colin Brydon and myself reinforced our belief that writing down problems in conventional symbolism would not help the children solve the problems. At the same time, it was surprising that none of the children generated an alternative representation based on one-to-one correspondence, such as drawing the icecreams or writing down dots.

Written representations of concrete problems based on the Box task

An opportunity arose some time later to extend this procedure to a group of sixteen 6-year-olds (range 5 years 7 months to 6 years 5 months). These children attended school in a severely deprived area of the city, and levels of achievement throughout the school were low. The procedure adopted with these children was similar to that described above, except that the children were seen individually by either Cathie Potts or myself. They were first presented with some concrete problems based on the Box task: they watched as bricks were added to or taken out of the box, and tried to work out how many bricks were in the box at the end. The problems increased in difficulty until the children were unable to work out the correct answer. At this point they were offered paper and pencil, and asked if this would help them solve the problem.

Out of the group of sixteen, only one child, Kelly-Ann, was able to take advantage of this offer.

CP: Seven bricks in the box, and five more put in. (Does so.) How many now?

Kelly-Ann: There was seven and you put three more?

CP: Five more.

Kelly-Ann: (Tries to work it out.) I don't know.

CP: Do you want a bit of paper? (Gives her one.)

Kelly-Ann: Seven, and then you put five in there. (Writes a reversed '7' and a '5', and then thinks for a while.) *Needing dots* [my emphasis]. (She divides the page with vertical lines, and draws the dots, as shown in figure 8.5.) I've put seven dots there and five dots there. (Counts all the dots.) Twelve!

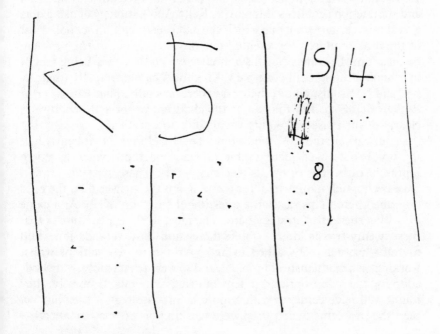

Figure 8.5   Kelly-Ann's dots

Kelly-Ann used a similar approach for representing the problem of four bricks removed from the box of twelve bricks. She divided up the page again and drew first twelve dots under the '12' and then four dots under the '4'. Then she remembered the original problem and said, 'Oh I don't do a four, eh? No, I put four out, eh?', and crossed out four of the dots in the group of twelve. She counted the remainder, 'Eight!', and wrote down the answer (see figure 8.5).

None of the other children produced anything like this when given the opportunity to use paper and pencil. The most common response – produced by well over half the children – was just to write down the numeral representing whatever they had guessed was the answer. One child wrote down numerals showing the initial quantity and the quantity put in, but guessed the answer; one wrote down a numeral for the number taken out; and one wrote down *all* the numerals from 1 to 11. Two children actually drew bricks: one drew the quantity she had guessed to be the answer, while the other drew a large (and apparently arbitrary) quantity.

These findings are quite striking. Altogether, Colin Brydon, Cathie Potts and I had seen a total of twenty-two 6-year-olds. Of these, only Kelly-Ann was able to use paper and pencil to solve difficult addition and subtraction problems. Moreover, Kelly-Ann's strategy of using dots was almost certainly not one which she had been taught in school. Most of the other children represented one or other aspect of the problem by means of the conventional symbolism which they *were* being taught in school, although only one pair (Kim and Leanne) actually used the ' + ' and ' – ' signs, and in their case there was talk about 'sums' prior to their doing so. For the rest of the children, paper and pencil were clearly of little use in helping them solve the problem.

In our earlier study, Miranda Jones and I had found that nearly half the 6-year-olds used pictographic or iconic methods when asked to represent quantities of bricks (see chapter 5). These strategies would have been much more useful for working out the answer than the ones described here. This raises the question of why only Kelly-Ann came up with a successful strategy here. The most likely explanation is that these twenty-two children – unlike those studied by Miranda Jones and myself – were actually asked to make written representations whilst working on a mathematical problem, and so were presumably *set* towards adopting the inappropriate strategy of using numerals. Ironically, they might well have come up with a more helpful strategy if they had *not* seen the problems which they were working on as 'mathematical'.

Translating from written to concrete

We also looked to see how these same children would respond when given written problems, in the conventional 'sum' format, which were slightly too difficult for them. Would they spontaneously translate these problems into an appropriate concrete representation, or would they – like the children studied earlier doing column subtraction problems – fail to benefit from the opportunity to use concrete materials?

The procedure was the reverse of the one just described. The children were given a series of written additions and subtractions which increased in difficulty until they started to make mistakes. At this point they were asked if they could think of anything that might help them solve the problems. On the table was a box of bricks which had already been used to give them concrete addition and subtraction problems. If the children did not mention the bricks, it was eventually suggested that they might be used. The procedure varied somewhat from child to child, as we attempted to match the problems to their own level of understanding.

The results were a mirror-image of the ones just discussed. Out of the twenty-two children, only three (one of whom was Kelly-Ann) made appropriate use of the bricks to solve a written problem. A further three children successfully used bricks to represent some of the elements of the problems, but failed to reach the correct answer. Most of the remaining children either refused to use the bricks at all, or used them in an apparently random manner.

Some of the children's responses revealed a major gap between their concrete and written understanding. Julie, for example, was given the problem '3 + 2 = ', and produced the answer '14', which she wrote down on her piece of paper. Her interviewer, Cathie Potts, suggested that she use the bricks. She counted out two groups of three and two bricks respectively, and then counted them: 'Five.'

CP: So which is the right answer?
Julie: Fourteen.
CP: Is it?
Julie: (Looks at her paper.) Coz three and two equals fourteen.
CP: That's what you've written, isn't it? But what answer do you get with the bricks?
Julie: Five. (She then miscounts all thirteen bricks on the table, including those not used in the addition.) Fourteen!

Somewhat surprisingly, Julie put more faith in her incorrect written methods than in her appropriate concrete strategy.

Another example was provided by Nadine. She was given the problem '7 − 4 =   ', and said 'Three'. She was asked if she wanted to check it with the bricks. She counted out a tower of seven bricks, and a row of four. She looked at the problem again and said 'Take away', so she moved the row of four out of the way. She counted the seven bricks remaining in the tower and wrote in the answer: '7 − 4 = 7'. She seemed quite happy with this result.

The most striking example of confusion about written and concrete representations came from Andrew. The problem was '13 − 5 =   '. He guessed 'Six' first of all, and was given the opportunity to use the bricks. He put out three groups, containing one, three and five bricks respectively. He then counted straight through and wrote down his answer: '9'.

Many of the children in fact had at their disposal a much more successful strategy for solving these written problems − that of using their fingers. Several children regularly used their fingers to work out the answer, and for numbers below ten they were almost invariably correct. Difficulties arose, not surprisingly, with numbers larger than ten. Nevertheless, some children produced various strategies for coping with these larger numbers.

Ian was one of the children who was interviewed by Colin Brydon and myself (see p. 128). He was asked to complete the sum '9 − 4 =   '. He worked it out on his fingers, and subsequently explained how he'd done it:

Ian: You start with ten (holds up ten fingers), put one down (does so), then put four down (does so), and you're left with five.
CB: How about this problem? (Writes down '11 − 4 =   '.)
Ian: (Works it out on his fingers.) Six!
CB: How did you do that?
Ian: (Holds up all ten fingers.) You pretend there's another finger, then you put four down, and then you count the rest.

Ian's strategy was an ingenious way of extending finger-counting beyond the basic ten. Unfortunately he had forgotten to count his pretend finger when working it out! Later, we asked him to do another written problem: '13 − 4'. Again, he produced the answer 'Six' and, again, he demonstrated using his fingers. This time he needed three pretend fingers and, as before, he forgot about them when counting how many were left at the end. Yet he seemed to have no other strategies available for working out problems in this range.

Our final example of an interesting finger-counting strategy came from

Mark, whom we discussed on page 128. He responded to the written problem '5 + 6 =   ' by laying one hand flat on the table, and saying 'Five'. He then laid a pencil down next to his hand. He put his other hand down on the other side of the pencil, and said 'Six'. Finally, he added up all eleven items (ten fingers and pencil), using his nose to count with! It was an extremely impressive performance.

Overview

In his book *Children's Arithmetic*, Herbert Ginsburg (1977) asks the following question and supplies his own answer (p. 125):

> Why do children have so much difficulty with written mathematics? Perhaps part of the answer is this. As we have seen, children's early and self-invented arithmetic mainly involves counting procedures applied to real objects. They usually count on their fingers to get a sum. Methods like this work easily and well. Next, children are taught various written procedures for accomplishing the same purposes. Unfortunately, they often fail to understand the necessity or rationale for written methods. Nevertheless, they are imposed on them and in school they are required to use them. The result is not only a bizarre written arithmetic, but a gap between it and children's informal knowledge.

The examples in this chapter provide very clear demonstrations of the point Ginsburg is making. We have seen young children using their fingers to solve simple problems, but failing when given the opportunity to use bricks. We have seen how conventional written symbolism, at this stage, does not help them. We have also seen that older children, at a stage in their arithmetic when written methods are not only helpful but essential, appear to have a seriously limited understanding of the written procedures they are using.

These examples also confirm the central importance of the idea of translation. The ability to translate appropriately and correctly between concrete and written representations of arithmetical problems appears to be fundamental to understanding arithmetic. Not only is it an integral part of the practical problem-solving advocated by Cockroft (see chapter 1), but it is needed in carrying out day-to-day exercises in the mathematics classroom. Yet it seems to be a continual source of difficulty for young children.

9

Learning through number games

We are faced, then, with a fundamental problem. Young children start school with a range of mathematical skills: they can, for example, work out simple additions and subtractions involving concrete objects, and they can invent meaningful ways of representing small quantities on paper. One of the tasks of school, however, is to introduce young children to a new kind of mathematical thinking. They must learn, among other things, how to use the conventional written symbols of arithmetic. And yet these symbols are not usually introduced in a way that helps young children to see the rationale for using them. As a result, children fail to establish connections – or translate – between this new kind of symbolism and their concrete understanding. At the very least, they will come to see written arithmetic as a system of rules and procedures divorced from concrete reality; at worst they will come to acquire a bizarre written arithmetic, like many of the chidren described in the last chapter.

In this chapter and the next we will be looking at new ways of introducing young children to formal arithmetical symbolism, ways which might avoid some of the problems we have just seen. We will start by looking at simple number games which can be played with such objects as dice, magnetic numerals and tobacco tins. In the next chapter we will look at a very different approach, using a micro-computer, a special keyboard and a floor-crawling robot called a Turtle. What unites these two approaches is that they both offer opportunities to introduce mathematical symbols to young children in ways that are interesting and enjoyable. They are intended, above all, to show that we can help children build meaningful links between the world of written symbols and the world of concrete reality.

Board-and-dice games

I have long been convinced that playing simple games is an ideal way to stimulate and motivate young children. I also believe that it is only when they *are* stimulated and motivated that children will realise their full potential. It was observing a young girl and her mother playing a game of knock-out whist which made me want to study in more detail how young children learn about number, and which led to my developing game-like problems, such as the Box task and the Tins game, as useful techniques in such an investigation.

One familiar category of games which rest very heavily on number are those involving a board and dice, such as snakes-and-ladders, Ludo and Monopoly. Nearly every child enjoys playing games of this kind, and it is surprising that they are not used more in teaching mathematics. My own particular interest in board-and-dice games concerned whether they could be used to develop pre-school children's understanding of written numerals. My idea was simple. First I would use ordinary dice (i.e. with dots) to familiarise children with the basic idea of the game. I would then use dice showing numerals instead of dots, so that the meaning of the numerals arose directly from the context of the game. I hoped that a child faced with a written '2' on a dice would see this as corresponding to two dots, and so translate easily between the *numeral* and the *number of dots*.

I devised an extremely simple game for playing with pre-school children. I drew a path on a large sheet of paper, and divided it into about thirty squares (see figure 9.1). I stuck the paper on to a low table and built two small houses out of cardboard: these were placed at each end of the path. The only materials needed were two small animals – a dog and a rabbit – and a variety of dice. I explained the game as follows. The dog and the rabbit started in one house and wanted to go along the path to the other ('to eat their dinners', as one child, Patrick, helpfully suggested). They could only do this if we threw the dice for the animals, counted the number of dots on the top, and then moved them the appropriate number of squares. The children could choose which animal to throw for, and I would throw for the other.

I played this game with twenty-two children from the Psychology Department Nursery, aged 3 years 5 months to 5 years 1 month. Because I wanted to know what each child would make of the game, I saw them individually (I imagine that most teachers would use games like this with small groups of children). About half the children claimed to have played games with dice before and were able to identify 'a dice'. One

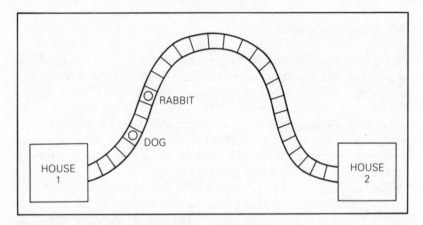

Figure 9.1   Layout of board-and-dice game

child quite reasonably referred to a dice as a 'domino', while another called it a 'rubber'.

The game was certainly very popular with the children: they would readily throw the dice, count the dots, and count out the required number of steps along the path. When the animals had reached the other house, virtually all the children wanted to play again. One child, Andrew, got so involved in the game that when his rabbit was 'winning' he would start cheering, gesticulating and waving his fist in triumph. He did not have to be asked whether he wanted a second game, but spontaneously said, 'I want to do it again!' Another child, Thomas, not only wanted to play again, but ended up throwing for both animals, and played out the return leg totally by himself.

Most of the children picked up the rules of the game very quickly. Several children, however, made the common mistake of counting out each move by starting with (i.e. calling 'one') the square on which their animal was standing. This meant that they were systematically depriving their animal of a square on each turn. The problem was particularly acute for a throw of 'one': Patrick, having made such a throw, tried to move his animal forward several times before eventually saying 'Stay back there!', and leaving it where it was.

Another common miscount occurred when a move took one animal past the other. On these occasions the children would frequently jump their animal over the other, thereby missing out (and not counting) the square on which the other animal was placed. Unlike the previous mistake, this one systematically gained their animal a square. This does not seem to be why they did it: the children in fact appeared to be motivated by the desire to prevent two animals from occupying the same square, although the squares were big enough to take them both.

I moved on with some of the older children (4- and 5-year-olds) to versions of the game which involved throwing two dice (see figure 9.2). We started with two dot-dice, and the children had to count up the overall number of dots. This presented few problems, provided we stayed within their counting range. Next, one of the dot-dice was replaced by a numeral-dice. Again, this caused little difficulty, although some of the children needed to be shown that it was easiest to start with the number shown on the numeral-dice and then count on the number of dots on the dot-dice. Thus, for a throw of '3' and two dots, they were encouraged to start with 'three' and then count on 'four, five'. Other children discovered this strategy for themselves, in a way reminiscent of children doing large-number versions of the Box task (see chapter 3). Finally, the children rolled two numeral-dice. For some of the children we were now getting out of their number range, and so for these children the numbers on the dice faces were limited to '1', '2' and '3'. (I constructed these dice out of small wooden bricks, rounding off the corners to help them roll.) However, even with small numbers, it was clear that the combination of two numerals was a frequent source of difficulty.

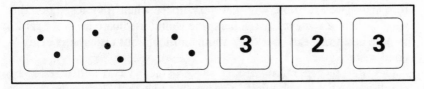

Figure 9.2   Dice used in the second version of the game

This difficulty was not unexpected, as successful addition of two numerals appears to require knowledge of the appropriate number fact. Thus, if a child throws a '3' and a '2', they will have problems unless they know that 'three and two makes five'. My interest here was in whether the children would be helped by the suggestion that the '2' stood for two dots, and the '3' for three dots. This approach, however, was fairly unsuccessful, as the following dialogue with Craig demonstrates. He had thrown a '3' and a '2', and had responded to this by saying 'Three, two', pointing to the appropriate dice.

MH: Three and two. Do you know how many that is altogether?
Craig: I don't know that.

MH: You don't know? Well, what if there were three spots on that
dice and two spots on that dice, what would there be altogether?
Craig: I don't know.
MH: If there were three on that dice and two on that?
Craig: (Just shakes head.)
MH: You don't know what three spots and two spots is?
Craig: No.
MH: Okay. (Demonstrates that the rabbit can be moved forward three
squares and then two further squares.)

Craig, it should be pointed out, had had little difficulty counting as many
as five spots when he rolled two dot-dice.

This brief experimentation with board-and-dice games shows that
they are a useful way of helping young children learn about number.
As well as being used to introduce numerals, they can also provide
children with a great deal of practice in counting and counting out:
the intrinsic motivation of the game means that children will readily
perform a large number of counts in a short space of time. Such games
can easily be extended to provide practice in a variety of basic addition
and subtraction principles. One has to be careful, however, with the
competitive aspect of these games: while many children are happy just
to play, there are some who get very upset when they lose. For this
reason, there may be many teachers who would use board-and-dice games
to help children learn not only about number, but also about being 'a
good loser'.

Despite the general success of these games, I was still puzzled by
children like Craig, who failed to grasp the idea that '2' on a dice meant
the same as two dots. It was possible, of course, that it was simply a
matter of familiarity, and that he only needed more practice with
numeral-dice to understand the idea. I was bothered, however, that there
was nothing *intrinsic to the game* which might have helped Craig translate
in his mind between '2' and two dots. It might have been better if the
'2' had been a removable label stuck over and hiding the two dots, so
that Craig could have checked his understanding of the numeral by
having a look underneath.

This last idea seemed very closely related to the Tins game, and
I decided to look at how that game could be used to introduce
conventional symbols. I was particularly attracted by the idea of
combining the Tins game with another idea – that of using magnetic
numerals.

Games with magnetic numerals

The magnetic numerals which I used are about 5 cm high, made of plastic, with small magnets embedded in their backs. They are available in most British toy shops. Sets of magnetic numerals usually contain operator signs such as ' + ', ' – ' and ' = '.

I was attracted by magnetic numerals because they have the unusual property of being both objects and symbols. They can be moved around and played with, while at the same time, they can be used to represent arithmetical concepts. Because of this dual property of magnetic numerals, it is not too difficult to devise games in which they serve as a doorway between the two worlds of concrete objects and mathematical symbols.

Before playing any games, I presented children from the Psychology Department Nursery with a large number of magnetic numerals to see what they would do with them. Some children sorted the magnetic numerals into sets, putting all the '1's together, all the '2's together and so on. Thomas, for example, collected together six '1's and put them in a row: he then placed a '6' underneath them, saying that the '6' went with the six '1's. Other children put numerals together to make new numbers which had meaning for them. Amanda put together a '1' and a '7' to make '17' and said that this was the number on her door, while Ram put together '1', '9', '8' and '0' to make the number for 'the month'.

Several children arranged the numerals in sequence from 1 to 9. This raises the interesting question of what they would do with zero ('0'). Some called it an 'O' ('oh'), and were not sure where to put it. Others called it a 'nothing' or 'zero' and put it either in front of the '1' or, less frequently, after the '9'. A few children put it after the '9' and said that it was a 'ten'. Finally there were those who put it after the '9', but said that it needed a 'one' to make it a 'ten'.

It was also interesting to see what happened if children were asked to count numerals laid out in sequence from '1' to '9'. Most children responded with their normal counting procedure, i.e. starting on the left and counting along the row. If their counting was accurate, they arrived at the total, 'nine', having counted every numeral in turn. Only a few children said 'Nine' without counting: they had realised that there must be nine numerals in the sequence, simply because it was complete.

Other children responded, quite unexpectedly, by starting their count at the *right-hand end*, saying 'one' as they touched the '9'. When this happened, their counting very quickly became confused, as they had the unusual experience of saying one number and touching a different one. It was puzzling that these children did not see the advantage of starting their count with the '1'.

Another idea which I found quite useful was to cover numerals at the beginning of the sequence with my hand. I then asked the children how many numerals were under my hand (see figure 9.3). Some children were completely stumped by this, and seemed to have no strategy for working out the answer. Other children were able to understand that if the sequence from 4 to 9 was visible then the sequence from 1 to 3 was covered: they could then work out that this sequence contained three numerals.

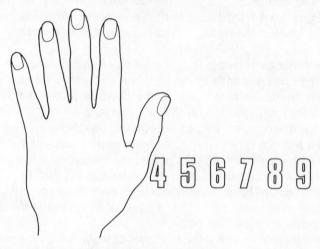

Figure 9.3 Partially covered sequence of numerals

A particularly impressive response to this problem was shown by Ram (4 years 7 months). In his case the numerals 1 to 5 were covered with a sheet of paper.

MH: How many numbers have I got covered up, do you know?
Ram: (Tries to look under paper.)
MH: You mustn't count them, just look at what's left.
Ram: Five, there must be.
MH: (Lifts paper.) Are you right?.
Ram: Wait a minute. (Gets me to replace paper. Thinks hard for a while.) Five, it's five. (Then allows me to take away paper.)
MH: (Covers all nine numerals with paper.) How many numbers have I got covered up now?
Ram: (At once) Nine!

What is noteworthy here is Ram's interest in the problem for its own sake. Having given his first answer, 'Five, there must be', he was allowed to see what was under the paper, but in fact he got me to replace the paper because he first wanted to be sure that he had correctly worked out the answer himself.

Magnetic numerals and the Tins game

These examples show that magnetic numerals can be used to present young children with a number of interesting puzzles. It is likely that they will learn a good deal from repeated exposure to such puzzles. I was particularly interested, however, in incorporating magnetic numerals into the Tins game described in chapter 5.

As before, I used four tins containing three, two, one and no bricks. The children were shown the contents of the tins, the lids were replaced, and the tins shuffled around. I then introduced a set of magnetic numerals and suggested that the children use them to help them remember how many bricks were in each tin. I was careful to avoid giving them any clues as to which numerals – or even how many numerals – they should put on each tin.

I played this version of the Tins game with twenty-five different children from the same school as before, matched as far as possible with the original twenty-five children. They responded with the same enthusiasm as the earlier group. Most of them readily used the magnetic numerals to help them identify the tins, and their use of these numerals did, indeed, help them play the game. Their initial level of success at identifying the tins was around chance but, after placing the numerals on the tins, over three-quarters of the pre-school group and all the class 1 group were completely successful. These scores were very similar to those obtained for written representations. As with the 'writing' group, they were just as successful at representing no bricks as they were at representing one, two and three bricks. They were also equally successful when retested a week later.

How did the children use the magnetic numerals to represent the contents of the tins? Their methods fell into three main categories: symbolic, iconic and idiosyncratic.

The most common kind of response was *symbolic*. Here the children used the magnetic numerals in a conventional way, sticking the '1' on the tin containing one brick, the '2' on the tin containing two bricks, and so on. Children using this method usually placed the '0' on the empty tin (see Jennifer in figure 9.4). Symbolic responses were used by every child in class 1, and by over half the pre-school group. Children using this method had no difficulty in identifying the tins from their representations, either at the time they made them or a week later.

Jennifer
(5 years 6 months)
(symbolic)

Marianne
(4 years 5 months)
(iconic)

Charlie
(3 years 3 months)
(idiosyncratic)

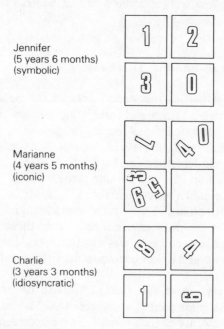

Figure 9.4 Uses of magnetic numerals in the Tins game

Four of the pre-school children made unexpected and imaginative use of the principle of one-to-one correspondence in representing the contents of the tins. Children using this *iconic* method placed one numeral, apparently chosen at random, on the tin containing one brick, two numerals on the tin containing two bricks, and three numerals on the tin containing three bricks (see Marianne in figure 9.4). Three of these children left the top of the empty tin blank, and one used an idiosyncratic '7'. Apart from one child who confused two and three, the children who used this method were successful at identifying the tins on the basis of their representations, both at the time they made them and a week later.

Finally, there were three pre-school children who used *idiosyncratic* methods. There seemed to be no clear pattern underlying the way they placed magnetic numerals on the tins (see Charlie in figure 9.4). I had anticipated that these idiosyncratic responders might be using a meaningful private code, but they were unable to recognise what they had done either at the time or a week later. As with the 'writing' group, they were encouraged on the second session to try again, but this did not help. However, when the iconic method of matching number of numerals to number of bricks was suggested to them, they all took it up with alacrity, and used it consistently.

These findings show that the Tins game is a successful and enjoyable way of demonstrating the use of numerals to young children. Certainly the children seemed to be getting the message that there were contexts in which numerals served an extremely useful purpose, and their comments were similar to those noted earlier: 'It's easy now coz we've stuck the numbers on.' Placing a magnetic numeral (or numerals) on top of a tin to represent the number of bricks inside the tin seemed an easy idea to grasp.

Adding tins together

I wanted to extend this idea further to introduce simple addition. Suppose that a child has placed a magnetic numeral '1' on a tin containing one brick and a magnetic numeral '2' on a tin containing two bricks. Suppose the two tins are now placed side by side. Is the child able to work out that there are three bricks altogether in the two tins and, if so, that this is equivalent to a tin showing the numeral '3'? This possibility seemed worth exploring, as it provides a nice demonstration of the equivalence of 'one and two' with 'three'.

This problem is superficially identical to the situation which arose in the board-and-dice game when two numeral-dice were rolled – the problem which caused Craig such difficulty earlier. There is, however, a crucial difference. Here the children have already grasped the essential relationship between the numbers of bricks in the boxes and the numerals which they themselves stuck on the lids: they undoubtedly *know the meaning* of the messages on the lids. This makes possible two strategies. First, the children might be able to visualise (if not actually remember) the bricks inside and somehow count them up. Secondly, if all else fails, the children can open the tin and have a look inside.

I found that most pre-school children have some initial difficulties with this set-up. The following interchange with Gavin (4 years 9 months) is typical. Gavin had produced a set of symbolic responses in the Tins game, and could identify each tin from the magnetic numeral on top. I then presented him with the layout of tins shown in figure 9.5. In front of him were the 2-tin and the 1-tin, and in front of me were the 0-tin and the 3-tin.

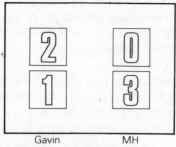

Figure 9.5   Layout of tins for Gavin and MH.

MH: Who's got more bricks, you or me?
Gavin: (Tapping his tins) I've got two and one.
MH: Yes, and how many have I got?
Gavin: Three and nothing. (Taps each of my tins.)
MH: So who's got more, you or me?
Gavin: Me. (Puts hand over his two tins.)
MH: Have you? How many have you got altogether?
Gavin: (Pause. Starts to open his tins.)
MH: No, don't have a look just yet. See if you can work it out. How
   many have you got?
Gavin: One in that tin and two in that tin? (Points to each tin.)
MH: Yes, so how many is that?
Gavin: Twelve.
MH: Twelve, mmm...that's more than me, isn't it? How many have
   I got?
Gavin: Nothing and...and...three.
MH: So you've got more than me, have you?
Gavin: Uh huh.

At this point I opened up the tins and asked Gavin to count how many
bricks were in each tin. Eventually he agreed that we had both got three
bricks.

Gavin seemed to understand the basic problem. He knew that he had
one brick and two bricks, and that I had three bricks and no bricks.
Yet he could not, in this situation, add up the contents of the tins.
Indeed, his response 'Twelve' suggests that he had got quite detached
from the context, and was operating according to the rule – which is
correct in other contexts – that 'one and two makes twelve'. Here, of
course, the rule is simply inappropriate.

Many children had initial difficulties similar to Gavin's. However,

I found that if I persisted they were sometimes able to succeed on this problem. In the following example, understanding comes quite dramatically to Debbie (4 years 11 months). Her problem was identical to Gavin's (see figure 9.5). I had in front of me the tins bearing the numerals '0' and '3', whereas she had the tins bearing the numerals '2' and '1'.

MH: Who has more, or do we both have the same?
Debbie: I've got the most.
MH: How many do you have?
Debbie: (Pause. Opens her tins and counts.) One...two...three. I've got three.
MH: And how many have I got?
Debbie: (Is about to open my tins when she exclaims in appreciation) Oh!...we've both got the same! (She then points to her tins) One...and two...*makes three*!

The expression on Debbie's face needed to be seen to be believed. It showed that she was having what psychologists have termed an '*Aha!*' experience, characterised by the sudden dawning of understanding. Her face lit up and she looked from the boxes away into the distance. This was clearly an important moment in Debbie's mathematical development, and I was fortunate to have observed it. The precise nature of her realisation is, however, less clear. She may have already been familiar with the expression 'One and two makes three', but was having a sudden glimpse of what that statement *meant* in this particular context. Alternatively, she might have suddenly realised that there was indeed an important relationship between the quantities 'one', 'two' and 'three', and had found a way of *expressing* the relationship in words. Either way, a crucial link was being forged.

I pursued this line of enquiry with my own son Owen (3 years 9 months). He was faced with exactly the same problem as Debbie and Gavin (see figure 9.5).

MH: Who's got more, me or you?
Owen: You? (Looks at me with a slight grin, uncertain.)
MH: You're not sure, are you? How could we find out who's got more bricks in their tins?
Owen: I don't know (rather doleful).
MH: You don't know how to find out?
Owen: No...(Looks at boxes. Suddenly looks up at me very alertly.) *We've both got the same*!

MH: Why do you think that?
Owen: Because *one* (picks up the '1' and puts it back) and *two more*
  (picks up the '2' and puts it back)!
MH: Is?
Owen: *Three*!

As with Debbie, Owen's face suddenly lit up as he made the connection
between the concrete situation and the abstract expression 'One...and
two more...is three.'
  I wanted to see how Owen would react if I moved an empty tin from
one person to the other.

MH: Now I'm going to give you that tin. (Moves the 0-tin over to
  Owen's side.) Who's got more now, you or me?
Owen: Me. (Then he makes a loud exploding sound as he realises he
  is wrong.) *We've both got the same*!

Owen clearly found it highly entertaining that we could move a tin from
one person to the other without changing the overall number of bricks
which we each possessed.
  These sessions with the Tins game showed that it is an extremely useful
way of helping children grasp some important mathematical ideas.
Indeed, these examples of Debbie and Owen suddenly realising one
aspect of the formal relationship between the numbers 'one', 'two' and
'three' are worth comparing with my unsuccessful attempts in chapter
4 to bring about this same realisation (see, for example, pp. 47–8).
Moreover, the Tins game can clearly be developed in many different
ways – for instance, to demonstrate that these relationships hold whether
the boxes contain bricks, beads, or any other kind of object. Yet the
basic idea on which the Tins game rests – that of placing written
symbols on the lids of tins – is extremely simple for young children
to grasp.

Introducing '+' and '−'

I wanted to see if the Tins game could be used to introduce pre-school
children to the operator signs '+' and '−'. These, as we saw earlier,
are a major cause of difficulty later on in school. For this reason some
people might feel it inappropriate to introduce them to children so young.
It seemed to me, though, that it might be possible to introduce them
in such a way that young children would easily grasp their meaning.

If so, then this not only would provide further insights into why older children find them difficult later on in school, but also might suggest ways of overcoming such difficulties.

What I had in mind was to combine the basic idea of the Box task described in chapter 3 with the use of magnetic numerals in the Tins game. My work with the Box task had shown that children aged 3 to 4 years knew that two bricks added to one in the box resulted in three bricks in the box. My subsequent work with the Tins game had also shown that they could grasp the idea of representing the initial contents of the box with a number on the lid. Could they also learn to represent the subsequent addition of two bricks with the sign ' + 2', so that the lid would then bear the message '1 + 2'? Moreover, would they then know that a tin bearing that message contained the same number of bricks as one bearing '3', or '2 + 1', or even '4 − 1'?

It was not easy to put this idea into practice. The main obstacle was that most children much preferred the single numeral '3' to the unnecessary collection '1 + 2'. However, I was encouraged by a few children who picked up the idea very quickly.

One such child was Thomas (4 years 0 months). We started with a '1' on a tin and one brick inside. The brick was in fact wrapped up in silver paper and referred to throughout as a 'sweet'. I explained that if I put one more sweet in the tin I would put the signs ' + ' and '1' on the lid, while if I put two sweets in I would show this with the signs ' + ' and '2'. I asked Thomas to shut his eyes, I put one more sweet in the tin, and I added the appropriate signs. The tin now had '1 + 1' on the lid.

MH: How many sweets in the tin now?
Thomas: (Guesses with eyes shut.) Three!
MH: Open your eyes!
Thomas: (Sees '1 + 1' on tin and seems to realise his guess was wrong.) I said three!
MH: How many sweets have I put in?
Thomas: Two...(Pause.)...One to begin with (points to the '1' on the left-hand side), and then you put in two (points to the '1' on the right-hand side).
MH: No I didn't.
Thomas: You put in one more.
MH: I put in one more.
Thomas: Which makes two! (Thomas replaces the '1 + 1' with a '2' and hides his eyes again. I put in two more sweets and add ' + 2' to the lid.)
MH: Open your eyes. How many have I put in this time?

Thomas: (Looks at '2 + 2'.) That means three. . .coz you started with
two and then you put in one. . .two. (Puzzles over the ' + 2'.)
MH: I put in two more, didn't I?
Thomas: You put in two more, so it makes four!

Clearly, Thomas had not totally grasped all the details of reading and
interpreting the signs on the tins. However, he seemed to have picked
up some of the ideas involved. He seemed to understand that a message
could be left behind to communicate information about something
that had happened in the past. He also seemed to be mastering the
convention that such messages are read from left to right. It is interesting
that he did not once refer to 'sweets', but instead used phrases like 'You
started with two', 'You put in two more' and 'It makes four.'

I decided to carry out a systematic study of whether pre-school children
could in fact understand arithmetical symbolism when introduced to
them in this way. I worked with twenty 4-year-old children (aged 4 years
1 month to 4 years 11 months) from two nursery schools in Edinburgh.
Ten of the children went to school in a working-class area severely
deprived of resources and amenities; their fathers had unskilled occupations or were unemployed, or absent. The other ten children attended
a school in a comfortable middle-class suburb; their fathers were all
employed in professional or managerial occupations. The children were
chosen at random from the available 4-year-olds in each school. (For
more details, see Hughes, 1983b.)

The children followed a programme which was structured but flexible.
This programme lasted for eight sessions over a period of six weeks.
The children were first introduced to the use of magnetic numerals in
the Tins game. They were then gradually introduced to the use of ' + '
and ' − ' to represent additions and subtractions. The following account
of how I introduced ' + 1' illustrates the general approach.

I produced three tins containing one, two and three bricks. On the
lids were the numerals which the child had put on during the previous
session. I took out a small teddy and explained that we would play a
game in which the teddy would put another brick in one of the tins
while the child's eyes were shut. When the child opened her eyes again,
she was asked to guess which tin the teddy had added a brick to.
Whichever tin she chose was opened and the contents compared with
what was on the lid. If the child could not work out whether or not
the teddy had added a brick, I helped her with questions like 'How
many bricks were in the tin before?', 'How many are in there now?'
and so on. This part of the game was repeated until the child seemed
to have grasped the idea.

I now introduced ' + ' (which I always called 'plus'). I explained that this was one of the teddy's special signs. He would use these signs to help the child. For example, if the teddy had added a brick to a particular tin, he would put ' + ' and '1' to the right of the numeral showing the contents. I would demonstrate this to the child and then play the game using these signs. When the child had correctly identified the tin to which the teddy had added a brick, I would ask her, 'How many bricks are inside now?' and so on. In later sessions I went on to introduce ' – 1', ' + 2' and ' – 2' in the same way.

A few children (five working-class, one middle-class) used the magnetic numerals in an iconic manner. For these children I adopted the convention that ' + ' meant that one had been added, ' – ' meant that one had been taken away, ' + + ' that two had been added, and ' – – ' that two had been taken away.

After a number of trials in which I manipulated the teddy, the roles were reversed and the child had an opportunity to play the teddy's role. This was an important part of the procedure and gave the child direct experience in handling the teddy, the symbols and the bricks. This was usually particularly enjoyable for the children.

This study showed very clearly that most 4-year-old children are capable of using and understanding a simple form of arithmetical symbolism in this way. All of them grasped the idea that the operator signs ' + ' and ' – ' could be used to indicate that a tin had had more bricks put in or some taken out, and almost all of them learnt the meanings of particular transformations such as ' + 2' and ' – 1'. In addition, the game was also thoroughly enjoyable. By the final session, the children were just as keen, if not keener, to come out for a game as they were at the beginning. At the same time, some aspects of the sessions were undoubtedly difficult, and many of the children acknowledged this with such comments as 'That's a hard one', or 'I don't know, I'll have to think about it.' This did not appear to detract from their enjoyment: many of the children seemed actually to appreciate intellectual problems pitched at the limits of their understanding in this way.

The method was almost inevitably more successful with some children than with others. In particular, while some of the working-class children made just as much progress as the middle-class children, others found it hard to grasp the nature of a message such as '1 + 2'. While they knew that the ' + ' meant that something had been added, they had difficulty in working out exactly what had taken place.

I was also interested in whether the children in both social-class groups could generalise what they had learned to new contexts. It turned out that even those children who had been most successful in using and understanding the operator signs throughout the games with the teddy, were unable to work out what these signs meant when they were used outside this game. For example, in one generalisation test they were asked to bang a tambourine '2 + 1' times. Even those children who knew immediately that '2 + 1' on a tin meant that there were now three bricks in the tin, were puzzled when they encountered '2 + 1' outside this context. It is not clear why the children did not make the connection between the two contexts. It is, of course, possible that they would have generalised if I had helped them see the links between the use of the symbols in the teddy game and their use in the context of banging the tambourine.

This study shows that it is after all possible to introduce the signs ' + ' and ' − ' to young children in a way they find both comprehensible and enjoyable. If a rationale can be found for using these symbols, and if a game can be constructed to demonstrate this rationale, then the majority of 4-year-olds are capable of learning the meaning of ' + ' and ' − '. This suggests that their subsequent difficulties in school are more to do with how these symbols are introduced and used than with any deeply rooted limitation in the children.

Overview

In this chapter we have looked at a variety of games which can be played with pre-school children. All of them introduce arithmetical symbols to children in contexts where the meaning is immediately clear and comprehensible. The children found them enjoyable and a great deal of learning appeared to be taking place. There were also some dramatic moments of insight, as when Debbie suddenly realised, when playing the Tins game, that 'One...and two...*makes three!*' At the same time, each game presented its own difficulties for the children. There were ideas or concepts involved in the games which several of the children did not at first find easy. This is perhaps only what we might expect: learning mathematics is not an easy process.

There is no reason why games like these cannot be used to develop an understanding of other aspects of the formal relationships between numbers. What is important is to keep in mind two fundamental principles, corresponding to the two 'directions' of translation. The first principle, corresponding to translation from concrete to symbolic representations of number, is that the games should introduce and use mathematical symbols in situations where they have an obvious meaning and where their usefulness can be clearly demonstrated. The second principle is that the games should allow and encourage children to translate from the symbols back to the corresponding concrete situation, whenever they need to check – or to work out – the answer to a problem.

10

Learning with LOGO

Some months after I carried out the work described in the last chapter, I became interested in how micro-computers might be used to help young children learn about number. The British government had just announced a scheme whereby every primary school in the country could obtain a half-price micro-computer, and a large amount of educational software was being produced in a variety of subject-areas. Much of the software fell into the general category of 'drill and practice', in which the computer is used to present sequences of sums to young children, giving the appropriate reinforcement according to their answer. There was, however, a growing school of thought which was critical of this use of the computer as an electronic work-card, and which maintained that children should not be on the receiving end of other people's programs, but should be writing their own. There was general agreement that the most common programming language, BASIC, was not the most appropriate one for children to learn. Instead, there was – and still is – growing interest in a language called LOGO, which has been developed specifically to help children to learn computer programming. The best-known advocate of LOGO is Seymour Papert, of the Massachusetts Institute of Technology, who has set out his arguments for LOGO in *Mindstorms: Children, Computers and Powerful Ideas* (1980).

Much of Papert's book is addressed to the problem with which I have myself been grappling – namely, how to introduce mathematics to children in ways that are both meaningful and motivating. One section in particular is very pertinent to my own concerns. In this section, Papert argues that current mathematics teaching inevitably leads to a dissociation between children's own interests and ideas, and the world of mathematics. Papert argues that we should respond to this problem by *reconstructing mathematics* in such a way as to make it 'appropriable', that is, more meaningful for young children and much easier for them to call their own. He writes (p. 54) that a number of principles have given more structure to the concept of an appropriable mathematics. First, there was the *continuity principle*: The mathematics must be continuous with well established personal knowledge from which it can inherit a sense of warmth and value as well as 'cognitive' competence. Then there was the *power principle*: It must empower the learner to perform personally meaningful projects that could not be done without it. Finally there was a *principle of cultural resonance*: The topic must make sense in terms of a larger social context....A dignified mathematics for children cannot be something we permit ourselves to inflict on children, like unpleasant medicine, although we see no reason to take it ourselves.

It was interesting to apply these three principles to the games described in the last chapter, involving tins, magnetic numbers and teddy bears. I felt reasonably satisfied that the games met Papert's first principle, the continuity principle. I had tried to build the games on to children's own personal knowledge, and hoped that the games had communicated a sense of warmth and value to them. I was less clear about the extent to which the games met Papert's second principle, the power principle. The games certainly gave the children a temporary power within the context of the games, and also gave them an introduction to a powerful tool: the language of mathematics. I doubted, however, whether the children had been introduced to a way of thinking, or to a language, which empowered them to 'perform personally meaningful projects that could not be done without it'. On the third principle, that of cultural resonance, I was also unclear. The games certainly made sense in themselves, but they did not necessarily resonate with other educational practices which the children would later encounter. Papert seemed to be implying that the programming language LOGO could satisfy his first two principles, if not the third. This suggested that LOGO might well be worth investigating as a possible further development of my own ideas.

What is LOGO?

LOGO is a computer programming language like BASIC, FORTRAN or PASCAL: in other words, it is a code which we use to tell a computer what to do. LOGO differs radically from these other languages, however, in that it was designed specifically for learning. It comes in several forms, of which the most attractive and best known is Turtle Graphics.

In Turtle Graphics the child uses LOGO to control the movements of a device called a Turtle. This Turtle can be either a small wheeled robot which can move about on the floor, or a tiny simulated Turtle on a computer screen. Both types of Turtle can leave a trail behind them (in the case of the former, by means of a pen). The child can thus instruct the Turtle to move around its environment in a particular way, and to produce a drawing or pattern as it does so. For example, if the child types the command FORWARD 100, the floor-Turtle will move forward 100 Turtle-steps (usually this would be a distance of around 50 cm). If the child now types the command RIGHT 90, the Turtle rotates clockwise through 90°. If the child types the further command FORWARD 100, the Turtle will move forward again, producing a right-angled corner (see figure 10.1).

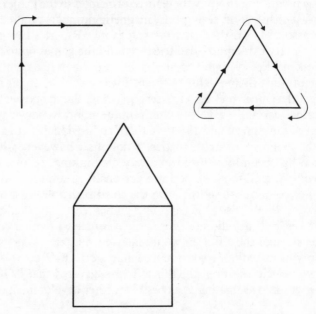

Figure 10.1   Right-angle, triangle and house drawn by the Turtle

One important feature of LOGO is the way in which *procedures* can be built up out of these sequences of commands. For example, the procedure TRIANGLE can be constructed by repeating three times the sequence: FORWARD 200, LEFT 120 (note that the external angle must be used – see figure 10.1). This procedure can then be stored in the computer's memory and retrieved by typing TRIANGLE. In turn, procedures such as TRIANGLE can themselves become building blocks for other procedures. For example, HOUSE can be constructed from SQUARE and TRIANGLE (figure 10.1).

The purpose of LOGO is not, of course, merely to provide children with a high-technology device for drawing houses. Its value lies in the kind of thinking children need to employ if they are to attain their objectives. In a typical LOGO session, children themselves decide upon a goal which they want to achieve. They then have to plan how to attain this goal, formulating the plan in such a way that it can be broken down into a sequence of Turtle instructions. This involves carrying out a number of translations from geometric shapes to formal LOGO commands. If the end result is not what the children intended, then they must reflect upon the deficiencies in their program and amend it accordingly. This process, known as 'debugging', is an important part of the LOGO philosophy: children are encouraged to see faulty programs as further problems to be solved.

The advantages which are claimed for LOGO thus lie in three different areas. First, there is the claim that LOGO, and particularly Turtle Graphics, can help children learn mathematical ideas. Producing Turtle drawings requires children to think mathematically in terms of distance and angle, as well as to perform logical calculations regarding how the drawings are to be produced. More specifically, it requires children to carry out translations between the concrete world of the Turtle and the formal language of LOGO, yet does so in a context where children can see very clearly the purpose of these translations. Secondly, LOGO can be seen as a stimulus for problem-solving. Producing a specific LOGO drawing requires a considerable amount of planning and problem-solving, which is not only valuable in itself but may also generalise to other areas of learning. Finally, there is the important argument that, with LOGO, computer technology is used to enhance children's creativity and thinking powers, rather than to constrain them into particular channels. 'Let the child control the computer, not the computer control the child' is Papert's message.

There is a certain amount of evidence that programming in LOGO has a beneficial effect on children's thinking, particularly in the area of mathematics (see, for example, reviews by Peter Ross and Jim Howe (1981), and by Roy Pea and Midian Kurland (1984)). However, there is little evidence as yet to support some of the more enthusiastic claims made about LOGO. Many advocates of LOGO would argue that it has never really been put to the test, and that we need to create LOGO 'micro-worlds' in which children have substantial access to microcomputers over long periods of time. If this were to happen, they claim, we would see major long-term effects on children's thinking and development.

LOGO and very young children

Up to now, LOGO has mostly been used with children aged 8 years or older. This is not surprising, given that Turtle Graphics requires an apparently sophisticated understanding of distance and rotation. It seemed to my colleague Hamish Macleod and myself, however, that a simplified version of LOGO could well be tried with much younger children. The idea of sending simple mathematical commands to control the floor-Turtle was likely to be attractive to young children: at the same time it would introduce them to a powerful use of formal mathematical symbolism.

Our first problem concerned the keyboard. The normal computer keyboard presents a bewildering array of keys to a young child, and so we used a special *Concept Keyboard*. This is a touch-sensitive pad which essentially allows teachers or researchers to design their own keyboard layouts. This meant that we could start with a very simple layout and increase its complexity as the children's proficiency with the system grew (figure 10.2).

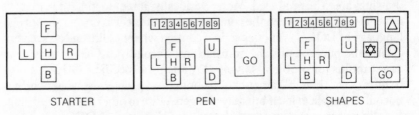

STARTER   PEN   SHAPES

Figure 10.2   Keyboard layouts

Our next concern was to simplify the commands used to control the floor-Turtle. We began with a very simple set-up called STARTER (see figure 10.2), in which pressing the key marked 'F' sent the Turtle forward one Turtle-length (about 28 cm). The command 'B' moved the Turtle back one Turtle-length, 'L' rotated it 90° to the left and 'R' rotated it 90° to the right. The fifth command used at this stage was 'H' (for 'hoot'): this caused the Turtle to play the first few bars of 'Scotland the Brave'.

The children next progressed to a more complex version called PEN (figure 10.2), in which the distance and rotation commands had to include a numeral (as in 'F 2' or 'R 3'), followed by pressing the 'GO' key, before the Turtle would move. The basic unit of rotation was 30°, so that 'L 1', for example, would turn the Turtle 30° to the left, and 'R 3' would turn it 90° to the right. The two remaining keys on the keyboard were 'U' and 'D': these caused the Turtle's pen to be in the 'up' (not writing) and 'down' (writing) positions respectively.

The next expansion of the system was called SHAPES (figure 10.2). This introduced the idea of pre-programmed shapes such as squares and triangles, with or without size-specifications: pressing '□ 2' followed by 'GO' would cause the Turtle to draw a square of side two Turtle-lengths. The final development allowed the children to move from controlling the floor-Turtle to controlling the screen-Turtle. They used the same keyboard layout as for SHAPES except that the 'H' was replaced by a 'CLEAR' key. This erased whatever was on the screen and returned the Turtle to its original position in the centre of the screen.

We tried out these simple versions of LOGO with five children, aged 4 years 2 months to 5 years 2 months, from the Psychology Department Nursery. None of the children had a computer at home. They worked with the Turtle in a separate room away from the main nursery. They usually came in pairs, although sometimes they were alone.

The children responded enthusiastically to the Turtle and were almost always eager to come out for a session. Once in the Turtle-room they sustained their interest for a substantial period of time: these sessions often lasted between twenty and thirty minutes and were usually ended by one of us rather than by them. This is indeed a long time for 4-year-old children to maintain their concentration, and demonstrates the considerable motivating power of the situation.

In the early sessions, the children used STARTER to control the floor-Turtle. They enjoyed moving the Turtle around the room and built paths and roads out of plastic bricks. They next moved on to PEN and produced drawings and patterns on large sheets of paper on the floor. In their last few sessions they moved on to the screen version of SHAPES.

In one of these sessions, Corrie and Susannah were experimenting with different shapes on the screen. In the set-up they were using, the prepared shapes were all a standard size. Susannah had discovered that she could make a 'flag' on the screen with the sequence: 'F 5', '□' (see figure 10.3a). I suggested she drew a lollipop, and drew one myself on some paper to demonstrate what I meant. Susannah did not immediately see how she could do this, but Corrie suggested they 'try a line and then a round'. So they tried 'F 5', '○', and were delighted with the result (figure 10.3b). They then experimented with different-sized sticks for their lollipop, discovering that 'F 1' gave a small stick, 'F 7' a larger one. Then they reversed the order of the commands: '○, 'F 5', and discovered that this led to an 'upside-down lollipop' (figure 10.3c).

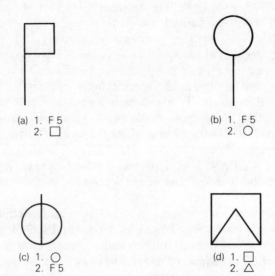

Figure 10.3   Screen-Turtle drawings by Corrie and Susannah: flag, lollipops, 'silly shape'

Susannah and Corrie carried on experimenting, and decided to make a 'silly shape'. Corrie suggested that they try 'square, triangle'. This reproduces an illustration from Papert's book *Mindstorms*, where a child trying to draw a house (triangle on top of square) produces this instead (figure 10.3d). When it appeared on the screen both girls burst into applause!

Apart from noting their obvious interest and enthusiasm, we did not carry out a systematic evaluation of this initial work with the nursery children. However, Muriel Slade, the teacher in charge of the nursery, spontaneously remarked that the Turtle work had had a noticeable effect on the confidence of these children. This effect was not simply the result of being taken out of the nursery to play games with an adult, for this was a normal occurrence for children in the Department Nursery. Rather, the effect seemed specific to the Turtle.

The Craigmillar LOGO Project

This experience with the Department Nursery children showed that our simplified version of LOGO was well worth taking further. We decided to introduce it to a group of children in Craigmillar Primary

School, in a severely deprived area of Edinburgh. Children in Craigmillar are very unlikely to have access to computers at home and, despite a hard-working and dedicated teaching staff, levels of achievement in the school are well below the national average. We felt that, if LOGO proved to be as beneficial to young children as we hoped, then the Craigmillar children deserved to be among the first to enjoy its benefits. We also wanted to reverse the more usual practice of carrying out innovatory projects with highly motivated and articulate children. Our motto was: 'If it works in Craigmillar, it'll work anywhere.'

Hamish Macleod, Cathie Potts and I worked for a period of five months with a group of fifteen children (nine boys, six girls) in their second year of primary school: their ages when we started ranged from 5 years 7 months to 6 years 5 months. In general, the children's number competence was well below average for their age, and our initial assessment of these children revealed many deficiencies in their understanding of arithmetic (see pp. 128–132). Indeed, despite the difference in age, the competence of these children was not much higher than that of the Department Nursery children described earlier. (For more details of the study, see Hughes, Macleod and Potts, 1986.)

The children were withdrawn from the classroom to a room which was given over to the project. Occasionally they came out individually, but usually it was in groups of two or three. Over the five months of the project each child received twenty-four sessions of about twenty minutes, resulting in around eight hours of contact with the computer. The method of working was semi-structured: the children decided at the start of each session what they were going to do with the Turtle, and then proceeded to carry out their plan, obtaining help when necessary.

The children first used STARTER to familiarise themselves with the Turtle and Concept Keyboard. The main activity for these sessions consisted of driving the Turtle around the floor of the Turtle-room. The children built houses and garages for the Turtle out of cardboard boxes, leaving large doors for the Turtle to move through. We also joined up these houses and garages by roads drawn on the floor with chalk: the children steered the Turtle along the roads, trying to keep within the chalk lines. The children's initial reaction to the set-up was one of great enthusiasm: 'It's barrie' (a term of extreme approval) was a commonly heard remark at this stage.

After four sessions, the children moved on to the PEN set-up. The Turtle was placed on a large plastic-coated board, allowing the children to draw either directly on the board itself, or on sheets of paper placed on the board. Initially, activities were suggested in which the Turtle moved from one location to another leaving a 'trail' behind it: attention was not focused explicitly on drawing pictures. In fact the children themselves soon started to attend to the shapes being produced by the Turtle.

After a few sessions with PEN, we introduced the idea of *planning*. We asked the children to make a plan of the drawing they wanted to produce with the Turtle, and discussed with them how the plan might be put into practice. As usual, the children reacted enthusiastically to this new idea, although their initial attempts bore little resemblance to anything that the Turtle might have been able to produce. However, their ability to produce realistic plans gradually improved with discussion and practice.

The pictures shown in figure 10.4 come from an early session with Julie, using PEN. She had seen some pictures of owls on her way along the corridor, and wanted to try to draw one with the Turtle. The first plan she produced (figure 10.4a) involved a circle and curved lines, and did not take account of the potential of the Turtle. After a brief discussion about the kinds of lines and shapes she had made with the Turtle before, Julie produced her second plan (figure 10.4b). This time she pointed out that the bird was made up of a square, a triangle, and straight lines. When she eventually came to operate the Turtle, Julie followed her plan quite carefully (figure 10.4c). She added the bird's face and wing by hand, and when asked whether or not owls had ears, she added the rather large ears.

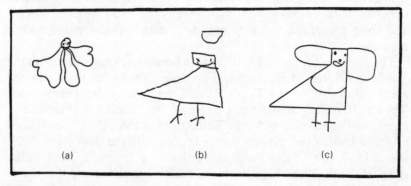

(a)   (b)   (c)

Figure 10.4 Owls by Julie

After six sessions with PEN the children moved on to SHAPES. This introduced them to pre-programmed shapes, such as the square, triangle, star and 'round'. The facility was obviously attractive to the children and it allowed them to produce more complex drawings. At the same time, it introduced new difficulties: for example, they had to learn the direction in which the Turtle would start off when making any particular shape, and had to plan accordingly.

The following extracts come from a session lasting forty minutes in which three boys used SHAPES to draw a snowman. The first extract starts after the Turtle had drawn the snowman's body. The boys had manoeuvred the Turtle into position to draw the snowman's head, but their first attempt had been 'too wee' (luckily the pen had not been lowered). Andrew replaced the Turtle in the exact position to start the head again, and they discussed what size to make it.

John: How big do you want it to be? One?...or two?...Dinnae press 'nine'!
Andrew: Three.
Kevin: Then 'GO'.
(The Turtle draws the head.)
John: That's quite a good snowman.
Kevin: Buttons.
Andrew: It'll be easy to make buttons, you just press 'one' and 'circle'.
Kevin: Hexagon, hexagon.

Andrew takes over from Kevin at the keyboard. He manoeuvres the Turtle to the middle of the snowman's body, although he has to be reminded that he must put the pen up first.

Kevin: Make buttons now.
Adult: What size are you going to make them?
Kevin: Small.
Andrew: Mmmmmm...one?
John: I say about one.

What the boys are doing here is *estimating* the likely effects of particular formal instructions, and planning accordingly. Estimation is not an easy skill to impart and, as we saw in chapter 1, many children reach the age of 13 or 14 years very limited in this respect. Here it follows on naturally from the activity of controlling the Turtle. The final result of the children's efforts is shown in figure 10.5.

For the last six sessions the children worked with the screen-Turtle. Some of the children were at first dismayed that the floor-Turtle was no longer being used, but most were curious about what the screen-Turtle could do. There was a new interest in experimenting with patterns – for example, exploring the effects of repeatedly trying the same shape,

Figure 10.5   Snowman by Andrew, Kevin and John

but with different sizes. As expected, it took the children some time to grasp the meaning of the commands 'U' and 'D' (pen up and pen down) in the screen context. However, there was little sign of the confusion we had expected between 'U'/'D' and 'F'/'B' (up/down the screen). Nor was there any problem about referring to the small triangle on the screen as the 'Turtle'.

The following session with Kelly-Ann and Lynn shows the flexibility of working with the screen-Turtle. Kelly-Ann started first, saying she was going to draw a rose: 'a big circle with wee ones all round'. She got as far as one large circle with two on its edge when she commented that it looked like a teddy bear and changed her plan (figure 10.6a).

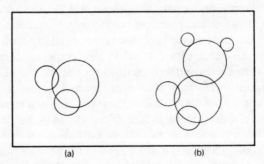

(a)   (b)

Figure 10.6   Teddy by Kelly-Ann and Lynn

Kelly-Ann and Lynn worked together on the positioning of the cursor to start the next large circle for the head. They both understood the value of trying a shape with the pen up at first, to check that it would appear in the right position. They added the head and a single ear, but had difficulty with the second ear. It was now several minutes into playtime, and Kelly-Ann asked, 'Could it no be a very old teddy and one ear fallen off?' Lynn was more persistent and added the final ear (figure 10.6b).

Evaluating the Craigmillar LOGO project

Our evaluation of the project occurred on two levels: the informal observations of the teachers who saw the project in operation, and the children's scores on a standardised ability test.

There was general agreement amongst all who observed the project that the Turtle work produced high levels of concentration from the children, and that this was almost entirely self-motivated:

> Their concentration – that's the thing that bowled me over the first time I saw it all. It still does. The number of them who stick at it and stick at it – it's amazing. And it's quite complicated – 'How do we get the Turtle up there?', 'Where do you want it to go?' You can almost *feel* the amount of concentration going in. (Headteacher)

> It's great, they really love it. The things that they're doing with the Turtle are much more advanced than when they started off. You know, they're really thinking. Like Craig, when he did that ship, he really thought about what he wanted and he explained it all: 'That's the ship, and that's the rail, the safety bars to hold you on, so you don't fall off' – and just the thought that's gone into the pictures. (Class teacher)

It was also very noticeable that the Turtle work stimulated the children's language, and particularly their use of mathematical terminology, as they discussed how to carry out a particular drawing:

> The children talk a lot about the Turtle work, especially when they're just back from a session. . . . They talk to each other more about the Turtle than about anything else. (Class teacher)

I certainly think their language has improved....If they hadn't been planning what they were doing then they wouldn't have been having the kind of communication they were having with each other....It's the sharing and discussion between themselves on the best way to go about something, which you don't even get in much older children in this school. (Head teacher)

There was some evidence that the Turtle work had helped children's mathematical understanding in the classroom, particularly in the area of number and shape. The class teacher had noticed

increased awareness of properties of shape – for example, that squares all have sides the same length. They now understand much more about angles, they know the meaning of big and small angles. They're also much better at estimating...and the layout of their work's much neater.

Finally, there was a feeling that the children who took part in the project were more confident and mature as a result of their experience:

I think they're more secure in themselves, more confident if you like. (Headteacher)

They're somehow more reasonable than the children of the same age who haven't had this experience. (Assistant headteacher)

They're much better now at working together in the classroom. (Class teacher)

At the beginning and end of the project, the children were all given a standard abilities test: the British Ability Scales. This test consists of a number of sub-scales measuring different abilities: the scores on the sub-scales can also be compiled to produce an overall IQ score. The sub-scales which we used covered areas such as non-verbal reasoning, vocabulary, matching shapes and basic number skills (counting, relative size and quantity, knowledge of more/same/less and simple addition and subtraction). Comparison of the children's scores before and after the project showed that they had made statistically significant gains on the three sub-scales concerned with number and shape. No significant gains were made on any of the other sub-scales (see Hughes et al., 1986, for more details). These gains suggest that the LOGO experience was having a measurable effect on the children's mathematical development.

Further analyses were carried out for the boys and girls separately. These revealed significant gains for the boys on two of the sub-scales concerned with number and shape; there was also, for the first time, a significant increase in overall IQ. There were, however, no significant gains for the girls on any of these measures, including IQ. This sex difference was unexpected, as the girls had apparently taken to the LOGO experience just as well as had the boys. One possible explanation is that the boys had lower initial scores than the girls and may therefore have had more to make up. However, it must be borne in mind that the number of girls in the sample was very small (six): further research is needed before we can make any definite statement that LOGO helps boys more than girls.

Overview

The version of LOGO which we developed has much to offer young children in their early attempts to understand mathematics. We have shown that LOGO can introduce mathematical ideas to children in a way that interests and stimulates them: indeed, the informal observations of the Craigmillar staff suggest that, when working with LOGO, children typically sustain an interest and involvement far beyond anything they produce elsewhere. Working with the Turtle makes young children think, it makes them discuss, it makes them explore and estimate, it makes them set themselves problems and discuss how to solve them, and it makes them use symbolic language in a way that is real and meaningful. It allows important links to be forged between the concrete world of the Turtle and the formal language of mathematics, and it provides a clear rationale for making these links. Moreover, the statistically significant gains found with the British Ability Scales suggest that the LOGO experience is having a substantial impact on their mathematical development – although these test scores do not tell us much about the nature of this impact.

Clearly there is considerable potential in LOGO. Yet there remain a number of problems to be solved before this potential can be fully realised in schools. There will be problems of space and classroom management if the Turtle is to be used in a normal classroom – something we were spared in the present study. There is the major question of resources: all this equipment costs money, a particularly short commodity in education. There is a problem reconciling the mathematics of LOGO – with its emphasis on distance, space and angle – with the mathematics currently used in many schools. The Craigmillar children, for example, were using concepts of angle considerably more advanced than those they encountered in their classroom. A further issue concerns progression within the LOGO language: by the end of the study, some of the children were ready for more complex LOGO ideas, such as the use of a 'repeat' facility, and procedure-building. The final problem concerns the development of appropriate teaching strategies. This is currently an area of considerable debate within LOGO circles, between those who advocate a highly structured interventionist approach and those who believe LOGO should be used with the minimum of adult guidance. The approach we adopted lies between these two extremes, but further research is needed to discover what kinds of adult intervention – if any – are most appropriate or useful in the LOGO learning process.

11

A new approach to number

We saw at the start of this book that there is increasing concern nowadays that children should not just learn basic mathematical skills, but should also understand how to apply their mathematical knowledge to solving practical problems. I suggested that there was a need for a new account of how young children learn about number, one which would avoid some of the pitfalls of Piaget's theory and throw light on why children's understanding of mathematics is often so limited. In this chapter I will consider the extent to which this aim has been achieved, and look at the implications for early mathematics education.

The competence of pre-school children

Piaget's theory has always emphasised the *lack* of competence in pre-school children – they are portrayed as egocentric, illogical and having an inadequate concept of number. In contrast, we have seen many examples in this book of young children displaying impressive mathematical abilities before they start school.

It now seems that most pre-school children can carry out simple additions and subtractions, often using appropriate counting strategies which may involve the assistance of their fingers. Most pre-school children can invent their own systems of written number notation, usually based on the fundamental principle of one-to-one correspondence, and can recognise and interpret these inventions up to a week after they have made them. Most pre-school children can use magnetic numerals to identify tins according to the number of objects inside, and will subsequently learn to use the magnetic symbols ' + ' and ' − ' in representing changes to the contents of the tins. Some pre-school children can even control the movements of a computer-driven Turtle robot by sending it simple mathematical commands. In none of these examples do children show the incoherence in their number concepts that a Piagetian might have predicted: they do not confuse number with length, or fail to understand one-to-one correspondence, or believe that addition and subtraction do not alter numerosity. Rather, within their limits, they appear to be competent users of number.

What are these limits? The most obvious one is that the abilities described above are usually restricted to small numbers (not more than three), although some pre-school children can cope with much larger numbers. A second limitation is that these abilities are not evenly distributed across all children: as a rule, children from relatively affluent middle-class areas are more competent than those from severely deprived areas, although the exact reasons for this disparity are not clear. Finally, and perhaps most importantly, the abilities of young children are most likely to be elicited by problems that arise naturally in a context which the children find interesting, and where the rationale for working out an answer, using a symbol or writing something down is clearly spelt out. As Margaret Donaldson has pointed out, their difficulties frequently start when they are required to move 'beyond the bounds of human sense'.

Any new approach to number must therefore recognise the fact that most children have an impressive range of mathematical abilities when they first start school. Yet this makes it even more puzzling that so many of them find school mathematics difficult and confusing. Even for the more competent children, mathematics often becomes a set of tricks and procedures which are applied fairly indiscriminately. There is a striking contrast between the lack of thought and care displayed by older children in their mathematics work at school (such as those seen in chapter 8), and the persistence and logic shown by much younger children as they grapple with mathematical problems before they start school. One has to ask: what is going wrong?

The nature of school mathematics

In school, children come to grips with a new and very different kind of mathematics. In previous articles (e.g. Hughes, 1983a) I have referred to this as the *formal code of arithmetic*, and indeed I often find it useful to think of mathematics as like a secret code, known only to those initiated into it. This code contains a number of features which distinguish it from the informal mathematics which children acquire before school. One essential feature is that it is *context-free*: it contains statements (such as "two and two makes four") which are not about any situation in particular, but which can be applied to a variety of situations, old and new. It also rests heavily on *written symbolism*

('2 + 2 = 4'). Both the written and the context-free nature of the formal code cause considerable difficulties for young children.

In the course of this book we have seen that mastering the formal code of arithmetic involves negotiating a complex of subtle and inter-related transitions. Some of these transitions can be distinguished: from actual to hypothetical situations, from concrete to abstract elements, from spoken to written language, from embedded to disembedded thought, from words to symbols and from the informal to the formal. This sequence is not intended to suggest any particular linear order, although clearly some transitions must precede others. At any stage in a child's mathematical development, they are therefore involved both in consolidating what they already understand, and in trying to link up the novel and unfamiliar with their existing state of knowledge.

I find it useful to think of these links in terms of *translating* from one form of representation to another. Usually these translations are not visible to the outsider, unless we specifically ask a child to carry out a translation task like those described in chapters 5, 7 and 8. There are some rare moments, however, when we may be fortunate enough to witness a crucial translation or linking taking place for the first time in a child's experience. The example which springs to mind is of 4-year-old Debbie (in chapter 9), who suddenly, during the Tins game, made some connection between the concrete quantities of one, two and three bricks, and the abstract statement 'one and two makes three'.

The concept of translation thus provides an important way of thinking about mathematical understanding. It can also help to redefine the problem posed at the start of the book. Those who emphasise the impor-tance of basic skills are thinking primarily of the ability to operate solely within the formal code, to carry out arithmetical computations and calculations free from any concrete realisations. This is undoubtedly an important part of being competent in mathematics. At the same time, we want children to do more than simply carry out computations: we want them to understand what they are doing, and to apply their know-ledge appropriately to practical problems. These problems do not usually present themselves in the appropriate mathematical form, but need to be translated into a formal representation before they can be solved. Similarly, it is frequently useful to translate a formal problem into a concrete representation in order to clarify whether we have understood it properly, or to check that a particular solution is reasonable, or to help us think about it when we are stuck. In order to solve practical mathematical problems, we need to be capable not only of operating within the formal code, but also of making fluent translations between formal and concrete representations of the same problem.

The difficulty of translation

The ability to translate fluently between different modes of representation is thus of paramount importance. Yet we have seen throughout this book that it is a constant source of difficulty for young children. We saw that very few pre-school children will spontaneously translate questions such as 'What does two and one make?' into concrete situations which they can understand (chapter 4). We have also seen that older children show a similar reluctance to translate in *either* direction between conventional written symbolism and concrete realisations, and that their readiness to translate is related to their mathematical ability rather than to their chronological age (chapters 5 and 7). Finally, we have seen that many of the difficulties which children have with mathematical problems in the classroom are closely related to problems in translating between the formal and the concrete (chapter 8).

Why is there this reluctance to translate? There are many possible reasons, but the following seems one of the most likely. Each of the translations just discussed can be seen as a bridge which must be crossed in order to get to the other side. While we as adults can see the advantages of being on the other side, the children themselves may not. They need to be *convinced* that the journey is worth making. Ideally they should be able to see that it will help them to accomplish a purpose of their own, or to solve a particular problem. Unfortunately, most of the time when we require children to carry out these translations, we do not also convince them in this way. Sometimes this may be because we simply lack the time to do so; on other occasions it may be because we find it hard to come up with a totally convincing rationale.

This point is well illustrated by the difficulties of making translations when children first encounter written symbolism. As we saw in chapter 9, *when children first encounter written arithmetic in school, it serves no obvious purpose*. It is not something which could possibly be perceived as a new and powerful tool, for it does not help at all with the simple concrete problems which children face at this age. If they cannot tell how many bricks result from adding five bricks to nine, then there is no advantage to be gained by writing down the problem as '9 + 5 =   ': this gets them no nearer the answer.

Indeed, it turns out that children's own invented notations are likely to be far more appropriate in these early stages than the conventional symbolism of arithmetic. The addition of nine bricks and five bricks is most usefully represented on paper, not by '9 + 5 =   ', but by an iconic method such as Kelly-Ann's dots (figure 8.5). Yet children are rarely encouraged to use these methods in school.

Whatever the source of children's translation difficulties might be, their consequences are undoubtedly profound. If children do not readily and fluently translate between different representations of mathematical problems, then a dangerous gap will develop. At best, this may simply mean that they will carry out their formal procedures competently but automatically, and with little understanding of their rationale or possible application. This would seem an accurate description of the way many children – and adults – perform arithmetic today. A much more damaging consequence is that their formal procedures will become faulty. Without any concrete underpinning, isolated mistakes can become habitual errors, and a bizarre written arithmetic can easily result.

The role of images in translation

The term 'translation' is useful in that it emphasises the linguistic aspects of mathematics. This does not mean, however, that visual aspects should be neglected: indeed, one frequently finds that visual images are amongst the most powerful means of providing a meaningful realisation of formal mathematics. Jerome Bruner and Helen Kenney (1974) studied the psychological processes involved in the learning of mathematics by a small group of very competent 8-year-olds. They commented (p. 433):

> what struck us about the children, as we observed them, is that they had not only understood the abstractions they had learned but also had a store of concrete images that served to exemplify the abstractions. When they searched for a way to deal with new problems, the task was usually carried out not simply by abstract means but also by matching up images.

This suggests that our understanding of learning and teaching mathematics might well be enhanced if we can identify those images and analogies which are particularly useful in connecting the formal and the concrete – and conversely those which are not. The biographical or autobiographical accounts of eminent mathematicians could be helpful here. Bill Higginson (1982) describes how four distinguished thinkers – Thomas Hobbes, Jean-Jacques Rousseau, Charles Darwin and Bertrand Russell – all had a positive feeling for geometry but an aversion to algebra. Higginson produces evidence from their own writings to argue that these men had problems with algebra because they failed to develop a strong image of the concepts involved, and thus responded to it purely at the symbolic level. He contrasts them with Einstein, whom he quotes as saying:

The words or the language, as they are written or spoken, do not seem to play any role in my mechanism of thought. The physical entities which seem to serve as elements in thought are certain signs and more or less clear images which can be 'voluntarily' reproduced and combined.

Higginson also notes that we have Seymour Papert's report in *Mindstorms* (1980) of the significant role played in his early mathematical understanding by images of gears. The young Papert, it seems, was entranced by gears and loved to think about their complex yet inter-connected movements. Papert indeed draws a strong parallel between his early love for gears and the attraction which many children feel for his creation, the Turtle. In Papert's terms, the Turtle is a *transitional device* which helps children link the formal and the concrete. The success of the Turtle emphasises the need for further devices of this kind.

A further stock of useful images surely exists in the everyday practice of successful teachers of early mathematics. In trying to put across diffi-cult ideas to children, many teachers will search their own intuitions and experience to find images or metaphors which will help – although some images, such as the one illustrated in figure 11.1, may not appeal to all readers. This expertise constitutes an extremely useful source, yet it is rarely made public and accessible.

Figure 11.1 Possible representation of subtraction problem
(from The Second Official I Hate Cats Book by Skip Morrow)

Instead, we have to rely on the accounts of researchers who have tried various devices or images with differing degrees of success. The Box task and Tins game described here are based around the simple idea of a closed box containing a number of objects. Changes can be made to the contents, and labels can be stuck on its lid to bear messages of various kinds. This idea seems to work well. A very similar device has been described by Robert Davis (1984) for introducing the concept of negative numbers. Davis uses a bag containing an unknown quantity of pebbles. At the start of the lesson four pebbles are added to the bag and the symbol '4' is written on the blackboard. Ten pebbles are then removed from the bag, and this is also written down.

$$\begin{array}{r} 4 \\ -10 \\ \hline \end{array}$$

The students are now likely to associate this problem's negative answer with the fact that there are six fewer pebbles in the bag than there were before.

I can recall how one of my own mathematics teachers, F. R. Watson, used the metaphor of 'money in the bank' for explaining positive and negative numbers. This helped me understand that, for example, if I had ' – £3' in the bank then I owed the bank £3. If I now took out a further £2, I would be even further in debt, and have ' – £3 – £2', or ' – £5'. These metaphors – which are essentially hypothetical concrete representations of formal mathematical symbolism – are important not only for introducing complex ideas, but also for helping us think about them and retain them in our minds.

It must also be remembered that children may develop images which are *not* useful. Richard Harvey (1982) reports the following surprising conversation with a child called David on the topic of odd and even numbers (I have made cosmetic changes to Harvey's original text).

David: Fifteen's odd and a half's even.
RH: Fifteen's odd and a half's even? Is it?
David: Yes.
RH: Why is a half even?
David: Because, erm, a quarter's odd and a half must be even.
RH: Why is a quarter odd?
David: Because it's only three.
RH: What's only three?
David: A quarter.
RH: A quarter's only three?
David: That's what I did in my division.

Harvey was at first unable to understand David's meaning. However, he was helped by a friend of David's, Robert, who put the image into words.

Robert: Yes, there's three parts in a quarter, like on a clock. It goes five, ten, fifteen.
RH: Oh I see.
Robert: There's only three parts in it.
RH: Ah, so you've got three lots of five minutes makes a quarter of an hour.
David: Yes. No. Yes, yes, yes.

Future research into the imagery and metaphors used in understanding mathematics should focus not only on which images are useful, but also on which must be guarded against. Children must learn to use some images and reject others, however appealing they may seem. This will require a conscious control over imagery, of the kind advocated by Einstein, so that the child controls the image instead of vice versa – by no means an easy task.

A theoretical shift in perspective

The conclusions presented here might be criticised on the grounds that they are based on new and hitherto untried methods, which have only been used with small numbers of children. Clearly, any attempt to improve on my methodology and replicate my findings with different groups of children would be welcome. At the same time, many of these findings are supported by recent research carried out in Switzerland by Anne and Hermine Sinclair, and in America by Rochel Gelman, Prentice Starkey, Barbara Allardice and Herbert Ginsburg. Much of this American research has been summarised by James Hiebert (1984), and his conclusions bear a striking resemblance to those put forward here:

> The thesis of this paper is that many children experience difficulty in learning school mathematics because its abstract and formal nature is much different from the intuitive and informal mathematics the children acquire...Much of school mathematics involves representing ideas with symbols and manipulating the symbols according to prescribed rules. Formalization is essential, but it also presents a serious learning and instructional problem. Many children do not connect the mathematical concepts and skills they

possess with the symbols and rules they are taught in school. I shall argue that it is the *absence* of these connections that induces the shift from intuitive and meaningful problem-solving approaches to mechanical and meaningless ones....

...Many of the children's observed difficulties can be described as a failure to link the understandings they already have with the symbols and rules they are expected to learn. Even though teachers illustrate the symbols and operations with pictures and objects, many children still have trouble establishing important links. (pp. 498, 501)

This emphasis on the difficult nature of learning mathematics makes a strong and important contrast with Piaget's argument that mathematical concepts occur naturally and spontaneously. Indeed, much of the thrust of recent research constitutes a marked theoretical shift away from the Piagetian position. Many of my own observations are in fact more in line with those of the Russian psychologist Lev Vygotsky. Of particular relevance is Vygotsky's idea that scientific and mathematical thinking should be regarded as tools, and his emphasis that 'writing should be meaningful for children, that an intrinsic need should be aroused in them, and that writing should be incorporated into a task that is necessary and relevant for life' (Vygotsky, 1978, p. 118).

The current theoretical shift also owes much to the work of Margaret Donaldson (1978), who emphasises the important transition in children's thinking from embedded to disembedded thinking. Indeed, it seems likely that the framework developed here might well be appropriate for considering other kinds of disembedded thinking. For example, it might be useful to consider the acquisition of formal logic in similar terms. Competence in formal logic would then be seen as characterised not only by correct manipulation of formal symbols, but also by fluent translation between formal thinking and concrete examples. As with early arithmetic, true competence would be marked by a clear understanding of which concrete analogies were appropriate and helpful, and which were not. This in turn would necessitate a degree of conscious control over the translation process.

Implications for early mathematics education

There is clearly much more to discover about the complex and fascinating business of learning mathematics. The findings reported here suggest the beginnings of a way forward, but do not constitute a fully worked-out classroom method. Nevertheless, they point to a number of areas in which a reorientation and rethinking is needed.

Redefine aims and objectives

We can start by offering a new perspective on the dialogue between those who emphasise the *formal manipulation of symbols* and those who emphasise the need for *concrete experience*. What seems clear is that both the formal and the concrete are important, and the child who has one without the other is at a serious disadvantage. Children need help in freeing their thinking from the concrete, and formalisation is essential in this process. At the same time, there is little virtue in children mastering the formal symbolism if the concrete understanding is lacking. The crucial new element introduced here is the emphasis on the *links between* the concrete and the formal. We need to redefine the aims and objectives of early mathematics education to give these links far more recognition than they have hitherto received.

Find out about children's mathematical background

How can these crucial links be fostered? An important first step for teachers of young children is to find out as much as they can about their children's mathematical background. Do they like numbers and counting? Do they ever play mathematical games at home – such as dice games or card games? Do they ever play with a calculator or a computer? Are there particular activities they like to do at home, such as cooking or shopping, which involve mathematical skills and where they appear to be knowledgeable? Clearly, parents will have to be relied upon to provide answers to most of these questions, and some teachers may feel wary about this: they may believe that parents often have widely inflated views about their own children's abilities. My experience, however, is that parents usually have a generally accurate picture of their own children, and are only too happy to be asked about their interests and favourite activities.

Build on children's own strategies

The next step is to recognise the informal and often untaught strategies which children possess when they start school, and which they use for solving simple number problems. These strategies – which make frequent use of fingers and counting up or down the number sequence – may not be totally reliable, but they are *meaningful* for young children and should be the basis from which mathematics education starts. Indeed, we could begin by helping children become better at using these strategies before introducing them to new ones: we could help them count forwards and backwards from a given number, show them how to use their fingers more effectively, and make the different methods of different children the focus of class discussion. We could even appreciate and encourage ingenious methods like those of Ian (p. 132), who used pretend fingers, and Mark (p. 133), who counted with his nose! Obviously, we want children to move on eventually to new and more powerful strategies, but, if these are forced upon children regardless of their own methods, they will not only fail to understand the new ones but will feel ashamed and defensive about their own.

Respect children's invented symbolism

Many teachers of early mathematics see young children having difficulty with the conventional written symbolism of arithmetic, and conclude, not surprisingly, that children in the first years of school are not yet ready for it. The research described here shows very clearly, however, that young children have a striking capacity for written symbolism even before they start school. As with children's informal methods of calculation, their own invented symbolism must be given much greater prominence in the classroom.

Children's early written representations of number are based on the fundamental principle of one-to-one correspondence. These representations are often ingenious and of considerable personal significance to children, and should be the basis of any early work on written symbolism. For example, it would be relatively easy to play the Tins game with a group of children, in the course of which different notations were used and compared. The children could then discuss why some methods were better than others, and might even spontaneously come to appreciate the advantages of having a common notation. This could lead on to the problem of representing numbers larger than those which could easily be managed with one-to-one correspondence, and thus the move towards a symbolic system based on numerals might make more sense to the children.

Similarly, work could be done with children's own representations of additions and subtractions before introducing them to the conventional plus and minus signs. As we have seen, young children find the representation of addition and subtraction very difficult, although they sometimes resort to 'action' methods using hands or arrows. Again, the advantages and disadvantages of these methods could be discussed by groups of children before the conventional system is introduced.

I have found no published accounts of this kind of approach being systematically used with very young children. However, a similar method used with 12-year-old children has been described by Nick James and John Mason (1982). These children were given the problem of working out how many blocks were needed to build a frame round a square picture of unknown size. The children were encouraged to develop different methods of representing the frame on paper, and then to develop different notations for expressing the number of bricks in the frame. Figure 11.2 shows the different methods adopted by two groups. It is interesting that one method led to the answer '4n + 4', while a different method led to the same answer, but expressed as $2(n+2) + 2n$.

Explain the history and purpose of conventional symbolism

There will clearly come a point when we will need to move beyond children's invented notation and introduce them to conventional symbolism. The key issue is not *when* this takes place, but *how* it is done. Two important principles need to be followed here.

First, we should be as *explicit* as possible in explaining to children what these symbols are called ('plus', 'equals', etc.), what they look like and why they are used. It may even help children to be given the historical background to these symbols. It may not be true that the signs '+' and '−' were originally used to mark excess or short amounts in warehouses, but we could certainly tell children that some people believe this to be so, thereby presenting a clear illustration of how such signs might be used. Similarly, children could also be told how the '=' was invented by Robert Recorde: his explanation for his choice of symbol (no two things being more equal) might well appeal to them.

Secondly, we should follow up this general introduction to symbols by using specific activities and problems which illustrate their particular use. Games like the Tins game or Teddy game described in chapter 9 would seem a good place to start. These games not only introduce children to numerals and operator signs, but also demonstrate ways in which these symbols can serve a useful purpose. It might even be possible to set up in the classroom a situation where children use messages such as '+ 1' to show that one piece of equipment is spare, or '− 3' to show that three are missing. The basic message that mathematical symbols can make life easier must be put across as frequently as possible; as Laurie Buxton (1982) points out: 'The answer is not to avoid mathematical symbols in a child's earlier experience. Rather one should capitalise on situations where the children feel a need for symbols.'

For Susan's Group the recording process looked like:

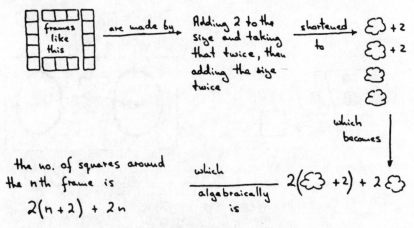

For Susan's Group:

frames
like
this
— are made / by taking → Size 4 times and adding 4 for the corners — shortened / to → ☁ × 4 / + 4

which became ↓

the no. of squares needed to surround a square picture of side n is:

$$4n + 4$$

← which, using the standard notations of algebra is   4 ☁ + 4

Similarly for Elizabeth's Group:

frames
like
this
— are made by → Adding 2 to the size and taking that twice, then adding the size twice — shortened / to → ☁ + 2 / ☁ + 2 / ☁ / ☁

which becomes ↓

the no. of squares around the nth frame is

$$2(n + 2) + 2n$$

which algebraically is $2(☁ + 2) + 2☁$

Figure 11.2 *Examples of recording processes*
(from James and Mason, 1982, p. 257: mistake in original corrected.)

Take particular care with non-standard symbolism

In this book I have given a considerable amount of attention to conventional notation (such as '3 + 4 = 7') which I was myself taught at school and which is still the most common form of notation. However, one of the by-products of the progressive mathematics movement of the 1960s was the introduction of several new types of notation. Many of these new methods use arrows to represent the operations of addition and subtraction. Given that arrows feature amongst children's spontaneously invented notations, it is possible that these methods are easier for children to understand. However, as far as I know, no systematic research has been carried out on this question.

Whichever notation is used, the basic principles remain the same, and a great deal of attention must be given to explaining the background and purpose of any notation used. Particular care needs to be taken if more than one non-standard notation is used at the same time. In the scheme produced by SPMG (Scottish Primary Mathematics Group), early work-books contain two different uses of arrows to represent addition alongside the conventional notation (see figure 11.3). In the long run it may be extremely beneficial for children to encounter and discuss the advantages and disadvantages of different systems. At the same time, it puts a considerable onus on the teacher to provide an adequate explanation for why these apparently confusing conventions are being used.

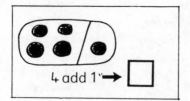
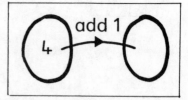

Figure 11.3   Representations of '4 + 1' in the SPMG scheme
(from SPMG, 1980, *Infant Mathematics: First Stage*, Books 4 and 5)

Use games rather than sums

Much of children's time in school is spent doing written exercises in the basic operations of addition, subtraction and so on. The main justification given for this is the need for children to practise their arithmetical skills. While there is clearly a need for such practice, the effect of carrying out so many purposeless calculations must be questioned. Games like those described in chapter 9 – using dice, or playing cards or dominoes – can provide just as much practice in basic skills, but in contexts which are both meaningful and enjoyable. One good source for number games is Herbert Kohl's book *Writing Maths and Games* (1977), in which he vividly describes how he used various number games to teach mathematics to black and Puerto Rican children in New York City. One interesting feature of Kohl's work is that the children themselves played a leading role in designing and making the games. Another useful source for number games is *40 Maths Games to Make and Play* by Margaret Williams and Heather Somerwill (1982). This book describes many different games involving boards, dice, cards and other props which can help children to count, to learn and practise 'number facts' and to increase their general proficiency with number.

Don't be afraid of explicit teaching

It may sometimes be necessary to spell out the relationship between written methods and concrete representations of these methods in a very explicit way. We saw several children in chapter 8 who tried unsuccessfully to connect the written procedure of 'decomposition' with the use of concrete materials, thereby revealing the weakness of their understanding of the procedure. In a recent American study, Lauren Resnick (cited in Resnick and Ford, 1981) describes a very specific method she used to explain these links to Leslie, a 9-year-old whose understanding was faulty. Resnick points out that 'The demonstration was accompanied by a thorough explanation of why each step was taken.' A sample of her method is shown in figure 11.4. Resnick reports that Leslie quickly learnt the rules. The blocks were then gradually faded out through a process in which the adult pretended to manipulate imaginary blocks, as directed by Leslie. Soon Leslie not only was solving problems in the conventional written form, but was also quick to understand when a slightly different method of notation was shown to her.

Training Procedure	Dienes Blocks Representation	
For the problem 85 − 47	Tens	Units
1. Represent the 85 with blocks.	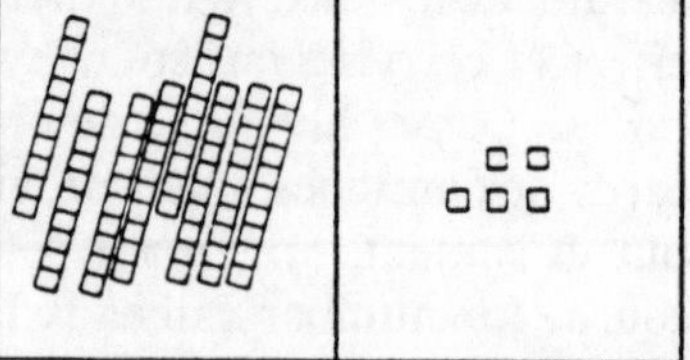	
2. Start in the ones column and try to remove the 7 blocks shown in the subtrahend. 3. There aren't enough blocks there, so go to the tens column and "borrow" a ten-bar. 4. On the written problem, cross out the 8, and write 7, to show the change in blocks in the tens column: $\frac{7\cancel{8}5}{-47}$	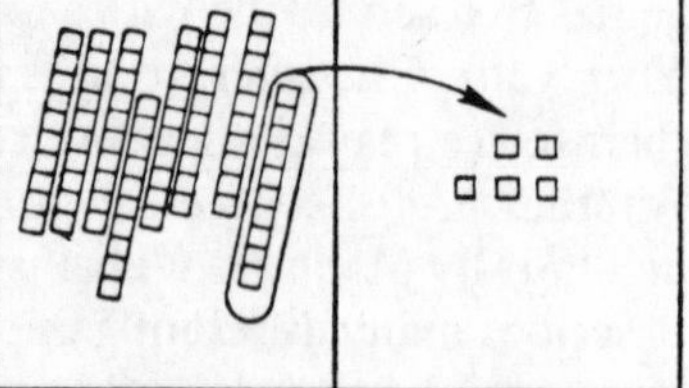	
5. Trade the ten-bar for 10 ones-cubes and place them in the ones column. 6. On the written problem, represent this by writing a 1 that changes the 5 to 15: $\frac{7\cancel{8}\,^{1}5}{-47}$	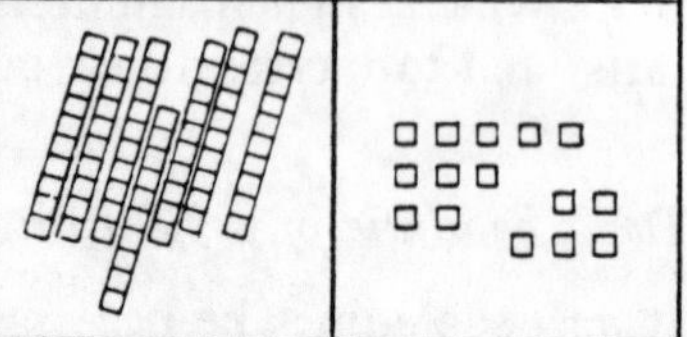	
7. Now remove the number of blocks shown in the ones column of the subtrahend. 8. Count the number of ones blocks remaining, and write the answer in the ones column of the written problem: $\frac{7\cancel{8}\,^{1}5}{\frac{-47}{8}}$	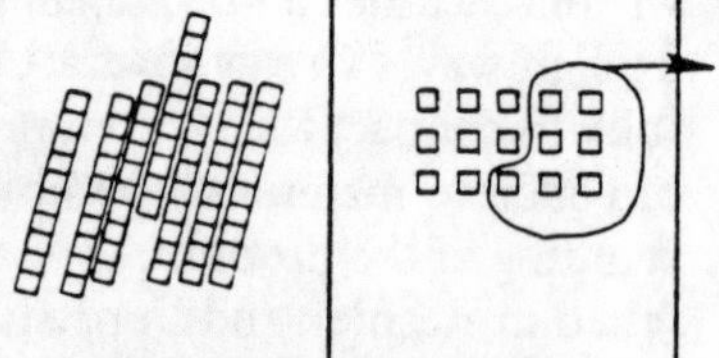	
9. Go to the tens column and try to remove the number of blocks shown in the subtrahend. 10. Since there are enough blocks, complete the operation, count the blocks remaining and write the answer in the tens column of the written problem: $\frac{7\cancel{8}\,^{1}5}{\frac{-47}{38}}$	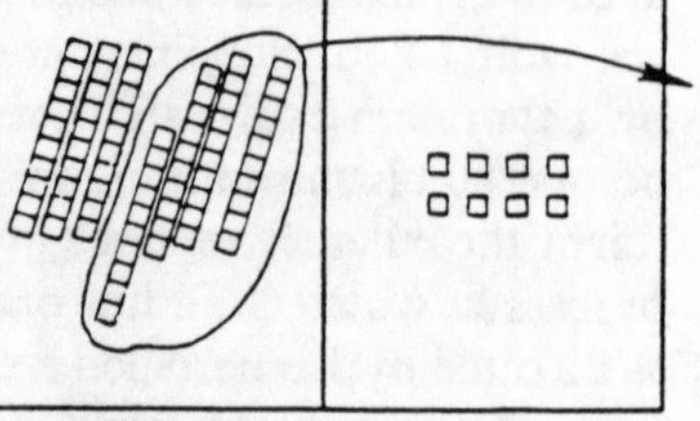	

Figure 11.4 Sample of procedure used by Lauren Resnick
(from L. B. Resnick and W. W. Ford, 1981, *The Psychology of Mathematics for Instruction*, (Lawrence Erlbaum Associates Inc.) p. 211)

Use new technology

The sudden availability of calculators and computers has caught many teachers by surprise, and there is still considerable resistance to the idea of using these devices with young children. This is unfortunate, given the enormous potential of new technology for helping children learn. Of particular interest is the approach embodied in the computer language LOGO. Not only does the production of Turtle Graphics provide an enjoyable and meaningful rationale for using a formal language, but the language itself empowers children in a way that conventional mathematics rarely does. LOGO will undoubtedly play an increasingly important role in early education. At the same time, it has its limits: we should not be aiming to replace mathematics with LOGO, but rather to use the ideas and principles of LOGO much more widely in mathematics teaching.

The changing nature of mathematics and the unchanging strengths of young children

In the course of this book we have looked not only at how children learn about number, but at different ways in which number can be represented. We have looked back nearly 30,000 years to one of the earliest-known representations of number scratched on a wolf-bone, and we have looked ahead to ways in which new technology might be used in the future. This historical perspective shows that there is no single unique subject called mathematics, but rather that it is a constantly evolving set of techniques, or tools, which human beings use to help them solve problems. The modes of representation and the way they are used are constantly changing. There is thus no single correct form of mathematics, nor a single correct method of teaching it.

The historical perspective also shows us that there is a continual trade-off between the power of mathematical tools and techniques, and the ease with which they can be grasped by those who are uninitiated in their use. Markings on bone, as we have seen, might be easily understood by all who knew to what they referred, but there are limitations to what can be achieved by this means. At the other end of the scale, the computer is a highly powerful device for carrying out an immense number of calculations, and yet for many people it is unapproachable and incomprehensible.

This poses a constant problem for those who teach mathematics to young children. We want to introduce children to the tools and techniques which form part of our culture and which we believe will help them solve the problems facing them. Yet, as these techniques grow more powerful, there is a danger that they will become less accessible to young children, and that teaching mathematics – already an immensely difficult task – will become even more demanding and time-consuming. Unless more resources are made available within the education system, pressure of circumstances will continue to make it exceedingly difficult for teachers to give new ideas, however important, the time and attention they deserve.

Clearly there is a challenge facing us. We have on our side, however, a strength which is often underestimated: the immense capacity of young children to grasp difficult ideas if they are presented in ways which interest them and make sense to them. It is not always easy to design situations which meet these criteria but, as I have tried to show in this book, the attempt to do so is usually worthwhile. If we can redesign our educational environments in the same way so that, instead of nullifying and ignoring young children's strengths, we are able to bring them into play and build on them, then I am confident that we will be able to meet the challenge currently facing us.

References

ACACE (Advisory Council for Adult and Continuing Education) – cited in
Cockroft, 1982.

Adda, J., 1982: Difficulties with mathematical symbolism: synonymy and
homonymy. *Visible Language*, *XVI*, 3, 205-214.

Allardice, B., 1977: The development of written representations for some
mathematical concepts. *Journal of Children's Mathematical Behaviour*, *1*, 4,
135-148.

Assessment of Performance Unit, 1980: *Mathematical Development. Primary
Survey Report No. 1*. London: HMSO.

Barker-Lunn, J., 1984: Junior school teachers: their methods and practices.
Educational Research, *26*, 3, 178–187.

Bede, the Venerable – cited in Flegg, 1984.

Behr, M., Erlwanger S., and Nichols, E., 1980: How children view the equals
sign. *Mathematics Teaching*, *92*, 13-15.

Bennett, N., Desforges, C., Cockburn A. and Wilkinson, B., 1984: *The Quality
of Pupil Learning Experiences*. London: Erlbaum.

Brannin, J., 1982: Cognitive factors in children's arithmetic errors. Paper
presented at NATO conference, Keele.

Brookes, W. M., 1980 (an unpublished study) – cited in Adda, 1982.

Brown, J. S., and Burton, R. R., 1978: Diagnostic models for procedural bugs
in basic mathematical skills. *Cognitive Science*, *2*, 2, 155-192.

Bruner, J. S., 1964: The course of cognitive growth. *American Psychologist*,
19, 1-15.

Bruner, J. S., and Kenney, H. J., 1974: Representation and mathematics
learning. In Bruner, J. S., *Beyond the Information Given: Studies in the
Psychology of Knowing*. London: Allen and Unwin.

Bryant, P. E., 1974: *Perception and Understanding in Young Children: An
Experimental Approach*. London: Methuen.

Buxton, L. G., 1982: Emotional responses to symbolism. *Visible Language*,
XVI, 3, 215-220.

Cajori, F., 1928: *A History of Mathematical Notations. Volume 1: Notations in
Elementary Mathematics*. La Salle, Ill.: Open Court.

Cockroft, W. H., 1982: (Chairman) *Mathematics Counts*. London: HMSO.

Cowan, R., 1979: Performance in number conservation tasks as a function of the number of items. *British Journal of Psychology*, 70, 77-81.

Davie, R., Butler, N., and Goldstein, H., 1972: *From Birth to Seven*. London: Longman.

Davis, R. B., 1984: *Learning Mathematics. The Cognitive Science Approach to Mathematics Education*. London: Croom Helm.

DES (Department of Education and Science), 1979: *Mathematics 5 to 11: A Handbook of Suggestions*. London: HMSO.

DES (Department of Education and Science), 1982: *Education 5 to 9: An Illustrative Survey of 80 First schools in England*. London: HMSO.

Descartes, R. – cited in Cajori, 1928.

Diophantus – cited in Cajori, 1928.

Dockrell, J., Campbell, R., and Neilson, I., 1980: Conservation accidents revisited. *International Journal of Behavioural Development*, 3, 423-439.

Donaldson, M., 1978: *Children's Minds*. London: Fontana.

Einstein, A. – cited in Higginson, 1982.

Ferreiro, E., 1978: What is written in a written sentence? A developmental answer. *Journal of Education*, 160, 25-39.

Flavell, J. H., 1963: *The Developmental Psychology of Jean Piaget*. Princeton, NJ: Van Nostrand.

Flegg, G., 1984: *Numbers: Their History and Meaning*. Harmondsworth: Penguin.

Fuson, K. C., 1982: An analysis of the counting-on solution procedure in addition. In Carpenter, T. P., Moser, J. M. and Romberg, T. A. (eds), *Addition and Subtraction: A Cognitive Perspective*. Hillsdale, NJ: Erlbaum.

Gelman, R., and Gallistel, C. R., 1978: *The Child's Understanding of Number*. Cambridge, Mass., and London: Harvard University Press.

Ginsburg, H. P., 1977: *Children's Arithmetic: the Learning Process*. New York: Van Nostrand.

Goethe, von – cited in Pimm, 1983.

Groen, G., and Kieran, C., 1983: The many faces of Piaget. In Ginsburg, H. P. (ed.), *The Development of Mathematical Thinking*. London: Academic Press.

Groen, G., and Resnick, L. B., 1977: Can preschool children invent addition algorithms? *Journal of Educational Psychology*, 69, 645-652.

Hart, K. M., 1981: (ed.) *Children's Understanding of Mathematics: 11-16*. London: John Murray.

Harvey, H. R., and Williams, B. J., 1980: Aztec arithmetic: positional notation and area calculation. *Science*, 210, 499-505.

Harvey, R., 1982: Learning in mathematics. In Torbe, M. (ed.), *Language, Teaching and Learning: Volume 6. Mathematics*. London: Ward Lock.

Hiebert, J., 1984: Children's mathematics learning: the struggle to link form and understanding. *The Elementary School Journal*, 84, 5, 497-513.

Higginson, W., 1982: Symbols, icons, and mathematical understanding. *Visible Language*, XVI, 3, 239-248.

Hooper, A., 1951: *The River Mathematics*. Edinburgh and London: Oliver and Boyd.

Hughes, M., 1981: Can pre-school children add and subtract? *Educational Psychology*, *1*, 207-219.

Hughes, M., 1983a: What is difficult about learning arithmetic? In Donaldson, M., Grieve, R., and Pratt, C. (eds), *Early Childhood: Development and Education*. Oxford: Basil Blackwell.

Hughes, M., 1983b: Teaching arithmetic to pre-school children. *Educational Review*, *35*, 2, 163-173.

Hughes, M. and Grieve, R., 1980: On asking children bizarre questions. *First Language*, *1*, 149-160.

Hughes, M., and Jones, M., 1986 (in press): Children's written representations of arithmetical concepts. In Thomson, G., and Donaldson, H. (eds), *New Directions in Educational Psychology*. Lewes: Falmer Press.

Hughes, M., Macleod, H., and Potts, C., 1986 (in press): Using LOGO with infant school children. *Educational Psychology*.

James, N., and Mason, J., 1982: Towards recording. *Visible Language*, *XVI*, 249-258.

Jones, M., 1981: Children's written representations of number and arithmetical operations. Unpublished MA thesis, University of Edinburgh.

Jones, M., 1982: Children's written representations of number and arithmetical operations in a communications task. Unpublished MSc. thesis, University of Edinburgh.

Klahr, D., and Wallace, J. G., 1973: The role of quantification operators in the development of conservation of quantity. *Cognitive Psychology*, *4*, 301-327.

Kohl, H., 1977: *Writing Maths and Games*. London: Methuen.

Litwin, M., 1984: Number and young children. Unpublished MA thesis, University of Western Australia.

Lyons, J., 1977: *Semantics*, Volume 1. Cambridge: Cambridge University Press.

McGarrigle, J., and Donaldson, M., 1974: Conservation accidents. *Cognition*, *3*, 341-350.

McGarrigle, J., Grieve, R., and Hughes, M., 1978: Interpreting inclusion: a contribution to the study of the child's cognitive and linguistic development. *Journal of Experimental Child Psychology*, *26*, 528-550.

Mathematical Association, 1956: *The Teaching of Mathematics in Primary Schools*. London: Bell.

Menninger, K., 1969: *Number Words and Number Symbols*. Cambridge, Mass.: MIT Press.

Morrow, S., 1980: *The Second Official I Hate Cats Book*, New York: Holt, Rinehart and Winston.

NAEP (National Assessment of Educational Progress), 1983: *The Third National Mathematics Assessment: Results, trends and issues*. Denver: Education Commission of the States.

Papert, S., 1980: *Mindstorms: Children, Computers and Powerful Ideas*. Brighton: Harvester.

Pea, R. D. and Kurland, D. M., 1984: On the cognitive effects of learning computer programming. *New Ideas in Psychology*, 2, 2, 137-168.

Peirce, C. S. – cited in Lyons, 1977.

Piaget, J., 1952: *The Child's Conception of Number*. London: Routledge and Kegan Paul.

Piaget, J., 1953: How children form mathematical concepts. *Scientific American*, 189, 5, 74-79.

Piaget, J., 1973: Comments on mathematical education. In Howson, A. G. (ed.), *Developments in Mathematical Education: Proceedings of the Second International Congress on Mathematical Education*. Cambridge: Cambridge University Press.

Pimm, D., 1983: Ambiguity has several meanings. Lecture given to the British Society for the Psychology of Learning Mathematics.

Popp, W., 1978: *History of Mathematics*. Milton Keynes: Open University Press.

Potts, C. A., 1983: Children's pencil and paper representations of simple objects in a 'Tins game' context. Unpublished MA thesis, University of Edinburgh.

Recorde, R., – cited in Cajori, 1928.

Resnick, L. B., and Ford, W. W., 1981: *The Psychology of Mathematics for Instruction*. Hillsdale, NJ: Erlbaum.

Ross P., and Howe, J. A. M., 1981: Teaching mathematics through programming: ten years on. In Lewis, R., and Tagg, D. (eds), *Computers in Education*. Amsterdam: North-Holland.

Saxe, G. B., 1979: Children's counting: the early formation of numerical symbols. *New Directions for Child Development*, 3, 73-84.

Schools Council, 1978: *Early Mathematical Experiences*. London: Addison-Wesley.

Schubauer-Leoni, M. L., and Perret-Clermont, A.-N., 1980: Interactions sociales et représentations symboliques dans le cadre de problèmes additifs. *Recherches en Didactique des Mathématiques*, 1, 3, 297-350.

Scottish Primary Mathematics Group (SPMG), 1980: *Infant Mathematics First Stage*, London: Heinemann.

Shuard, H., 1983: Discussion and the teaching of mathematics. *Educational Analysis*, 5, 3, 15-32.

Shuard, H., 1984: Mathematics in English primary schools. *The Elementary School Journal*, 84, 5, 583-594.

Sinclair, A., 1984: Three year olds' writing behaviours. Paper presented at the Third International Congress for the Study of Child Language, Austin, Texas.

Sinclair, A., Siegrist, F. and Sinclair, H., 1983: Young children's ideas about the written number system. In Rogers, D., and Sloboda, J. (eds), *The Acquisition of Symbolic Skills*. New York: Plenum.

Sinclair, A. and Sinclair, H., 1984: Preschool children's interpretation of written numbers. *Human Learning*, 3, 173-184.

Skemp, R. R., 1971: *The Psychology of Learning Mathematics*. Harmondsworth: Penguin.

Stallard, A., 1982: Children's understanding of written arithmetical symbolism. Unpublished MA thesis, University of Edinburgh.

Starkey, P., 1983: Some precursors of early arithmetic competencies. Paper presented at the Biennial Meeting of the Society for Research in Child Development, Detroit.

Starkey, P., and Gelman, R., 1982: The development of addition and subtraction abilities prior to formal schooling in arithmetic. In Carpenter, T. P., Moser, J. M., and Romberg, T. A., (eds), *Addition and subtraction: A Cognitive Perspective*. Hillsdale, NJ: Erlbaum.

Thorndike, E. L., 1922: *The Psychology of Arithmetic*. New York: Macmillan.

Tizard, B., and Hughes, M., 1984: *Young Children Learning*. London: Fontana.

VanLehn, K., 1983: On the representation of procedures in repair theory. In Ginsburg, H. P., (ed.) *The Development of Mathematical Thinking*. London: Academic Press.

Vygotsky, L. S., 1978: *Mind and Society: The Development of Higher Psychological Processes*. Cambridge, Mass.: Harvard University Press.

Williams, M., and Somerwill, H., 1982: *40 Maths Games to Make and Play*. London and Basingstoke: Macmillan.

Young, A. W., and McPherson, J., 1976: Ways of making number judgments and children's understanding of quantity relations. *British Journal of Educational Psychology*, *46*, 328-332.

Zaslavsky, C., 1973: *Africa Counts*. Boston, Mass.: Prindle, Weber and Schmidt.

Index

abstract and concrete linked, 44–51
abstraction, 39–41
Adda, J., 110–11
addition
  and class-inclusion, 15
  column addition, 121
  in Egyptian number system, 91
  of fractions, 7
  pre-school, 24–36
  with Tins game, 143–6
  with two dice, 137–8
  use of concrete materials in, 131,
    133
  written representations of, 72–7, 78,
    92–94, 121, 123 fig., 124, 128–30
  see also operator signs
Advisory Council for Adult and
  Continuing Education, 3
algebra, 111
Allardice, B., 54, 77, 174
application of mathematics, 3–4, 9
  see also translating
arithmetical symbolism, see formal
  symbolism
Assessment of Performance Unit, 4–5
Aztec system of notation, 90

Babylonian system of notation, 85, 86, 89
  'minus', 91
  zero symbol, 89
Barker-Lunn, J., 9
base (of number system), 82, 86
BASIC, 152
basic skills, 3, 169
  over-emphasised in classroom, 8,
    9–10

Bede, the Venerable, 81 fig., 82
behaviourism, 17–18, 44
Behr, M., 110
Bennett, N., 9
bizarre questions, 46
body-parts used in counting, 80, 82,
    83 fig.
  see also finger-counting
Botocudos tribe, number-words, 82
Box task, 25–32, 34–5, 38–9
Brannin, J., 118
British Ability Scales, 164–5
Brookes, W. M., 110–11
Brown, J. S., 115
Bruner, J. S., 60, 171
Bryant, P. E., 19
Brydon, C., 124–8, 132
Burton, R. R., 115
bus problem, 7, 44
Butler, N., 32
Buxton, L. G., 178

Cajori, F., 80, 86, 90, 91, 92
calculators, 1, 4, 7, 111
Campbell, R., 20
children's representations
  of addition and subtraction: by
    writing or drawing, 72–7, 78,
    129–30
  of quantity: by writing or drawing,
    54–72, 77–8; with magnetic
    numerals, 141–3
  of zero: by writing or drawing,
    62–3, 65–6, 77–8; with magnetic
    numerals, 141–2
cipherisation, 86, 87–8

class differences, 32–4
class-inclusion, 14–15, 19–20, 21, 22
Cockroft, W. H., 2
Cockroft committee, 2–4, 9, 42
colour concepts, 41, 46
communication tasks, 76–7
Complete Operations task, 72–3, 74
computers, 1, 152, 183
  see also LOGO
Concept Keyboard, 156
conservation, 14, 15–17, 19, 20, 21, 22
counting-on strategy, 28, 30, 32, 35,
  137
Cowan, R., 27–8
Craigmillar LOGO Project, 158–66
  evaluation, 163–6
cultural differences, see other cultures
cuneiform script, see Babylonian system
  of notation

Darwin, C., 171
Davie, R., 32
Davis, R. B., 44, 173
demotic script, 86–7
Department of Education and Science,
  8, 9
Descartes, R., sign for zero, 92
Dienes Multi-base Arithmetic Blocks,
  116, 182 fig.
difficulties, children's
  in school, 113–33, 174–5
  sources of: abstractness, 38–41,
    44–8; column subtraction,
    113–21; new language, 42–4, 45;
    new use for familiar words, 37–8,
    42–3; place-value, 121–2
  see also translation
Diophantus, minus sign, 92
disembedded thinking, 21, 175
division, 4–5, 7
Dockrell, J., 20
Donaldson, M., viii, 13, 19, 20, 21,
  168, 175

Egyptian system of notation, 85, 86–7
  addition and subtraction, 91
  'equals', 92
Einstein, A., 171–2
embedded thinking, 21
equals, see operator signs

Erlwanger, S., 110
estimation, 7

familiar words used in arithmetic, 37–8,
  42–3
Ferreiro, E., 93
finger-counting, 28, 30, 34
  elaborated, 81 fig., 82, 132–3
  to be encouraged in school, 177
  failure in using, 122
  linking abstract and concrete, 48–51
  similarity to tallying, 61
  used universally, 80–2
Flavell, J. H., 13
Flegg, G., 80, 81 fig., 83, 84 fig., 90
formal language, 31–2
  see also formal symbolism
formal symbolism
  children's understanding of, 95–112
  context-free nature of, 168–9
  difficult to master, 174–5
  need for rationale for using, 122–30,
    134, 170
  Piagetian attitude to, 17–18
  recommended approach to, 176–83
  see also disembedded thinking and
    operator signs
fractions, 7
Fuson, K. C., 35

Gallistel, C. R., 19, 27–8
Gallup Poll, 3
games, 134–8, 150–1, 153, 181
  board-and-dice, 135–8
  knockout whist, ix
  with magnetic numerals, 139–41
  see also Tins game
Gelman, R., 19, 20–1, 27–8, 34, 174
generalisation of '2 + 1', 150
Ginsburg, H. P., 121–2, 133, 174
Goethe, 42
Goldstein, H., 32
Greek system of notation, 87–8
Grieve, R., 46
Groen, G. J., 22, 35

Hart, K. M., 5
Harvey, H. R., 90
Harvey, R., 173–4
Her Majesty's Inspectorate, surveys, 8, 9

Hiebert, J., 7, 174–5
hieratic script, 86, 87 fig.
hieroglyphics, 85, 86–7, 91
Higginson, W., 171–2
Hindu system of notation, 88, 90
Hindu-Arabic system of notation, 90
Hobbes, T., 171
Hooper, A., 83
Howe, J. A. M., 155
hypothetical questions, 31–2, 38, 40–1

iconic response category, 58, 60
idiosyncratic response category, 56–7
images, 171–4
    see also visualising
invariance of number, 20–1

James, N., 178, 179 fig.
Jones, M., 54–61, 62–3, 72–5, 76–7

Kenney, H. J., 171
Kieran, C., 22
Klahr, D., 28
Kohl, H., 181
Kurland, D. M., 155

Leupold, 81 fig.
Litwin, M., 77
LOGO, ix, 152–66, 183
    Concept Keyboard, 156
    Craigmillar LOGO Project, 158–66
    debugging, 155
    PEN, 156–7, 159–60
    and pre-school children, 156–8
    procedures, 154–5
    screen-Turtle, 154, 161–3
    SHAPES, 157, 160–3
    STARTER, 156, 157, 159
    Turtle Graphics, 153–66, 183
Lyons, J., 60

McGarrigle, J., 19–20
Macleod, H., ix, 156–65
McPherson, J., 27–8
magnetic numerals, 139–50
    and adding tins together, 143–6
    and Tins game, 141–3
Mason, J., 178, 179 fig.

mathematical abilities
    of adults, 3, 110–11
    of 11- to 13-year-olds, 4–6, 7, 8
    pre-school, see pre-school children
    of school-leavers, 2
mathematical ability related to
    translating, 108–9
Mathematical Association, 8
mathematics
    changing nature of, 183–4
    education, see school mathematics
    as a language, 41–4, 48–9; see also
        translating
    negative feelings towards, ix–x, 2–3
Matthews, G., 24
Matthews, J., 24
Mayan system of notation, 90
Menninger, K., 48
minus, see operator signs
Morrow, S., 172 fig.
multiplication, 7, 46–7

National Assessment of Educational
    Progress, 6–7
National Child Development Study, 32
National Foundation for Educational
    Research, 9
Naughty Teddy, 20
Neilson, I., 20
Nichols, E., 110
non-standard methods 36, 123, 170–1,
    176–7
    of adults, 3
    'building up', 6
    counting on, 35
    Kelly-Ann's dots, 130
    see also finger-counting and
        children's representations
Nuffield Primary Mathematics
    Project, 8
number games, see games
number systems, 79–94
    Aztec, 90
    Babylonian, 85, 86, 89, 91
    Egyptian, 85, 86–7
    Greek, 87–8
    Hindu, 88, 90
    Hindu-Arabic, 90
    Mayan, 90
    order used in, 86

our own, 82, 88
place-value in, 85, 89–90
Roman, 85–6
zero in, 89–90
number words, 48, 80, 82
numbers
negative, 173
odd and even, 173–4
numerals
on dice, 137–8
in the environment, 95–7
evolution of 86–8
magnetic, 139–46
sequence of, 139–41
nursery school, effect of, 33

Oksapmin tribe, 82, 83 fig.
one-to-one correspondence
in children's representations, 58, 77, 177
fundamental to tallying, 82–4
suggested as strategy, 71–2, 143
traces of in our numerals, 88
transition to symbolic method, 177
in use of fingers, 82
usefulness of as method, 123 fig., 124, 125 fig., 142
'ontogeny recapitulates phylogeny', 79, 92–3, 94
operator signs '+', '−' and '='
children's explanations of, 103–8
children's reluctance to use, 74–5, 77, 78, 130
children's understanding of, 5–6, 98, 100–3, 109–11
in the environment, 96–7
in 'incomplete sums', 102–3, 107
introduction of to pre-school children, 146–51
origins of, 92
in other cultures, 90–2
in 'reversed' sums, 108, 110
understood as instructions, 109–11
'3 = 3', 108
other cultures, 79–94
addition, subtraction and equality in, 90–2, 93–4
Botocudos number words, 82
developments from tallying, 85–6
early Indian number words, 48

evolution of numerals, 86–8
finger-counting, 80–2
place-value and zero, 89–90
tallies, 83–4
see also number systems

Papert, S., 152–3, 172
Pea, R. D., 155
Peanuts cartoon, 42, 43 fig., 88
Peet, T. E., 91
Peirce, C. S., 60
Perret-Clermont, A. N., 77
Piaget, J.
criticised, 12–23
relevance of, 22
theory of intellectual development, 12–14, 40, 79
underpinning progressivism, 10, 18
views on capabilities of young children, viii, 36, 167
views on mathematics education, 12–13, 16–17, 18, 22–4
see also class-inclusion and conservation
Piagetian activities, 17, 18
pictographic response category, 57–8
Pile task, 73–5, 76–7, 102
Pimm, D., 43, 84
place-value, 85, 89–90, 121
and zero, 89–90
plus, see operator signs
Popp, W., 82
Potts, C. A., 77, 128–30, 131, 159–65
pre-school children, ix, 19–21, 24–36, 134–51, 156–8, 167–8
adding and subtracting, 24–36;
assessed by reaching behaviour, 34–5; with board-and-dice games, 137–8; with Box task, 25–31; with hypothetical questions, 31–2; with Tins game, 143–6
and class-inclusion, 19–20
and conservation, 20–1
counting on, 28, 30, 35, 137
finger-counting, 48–51
introduced to '+' and '−', 146–50
miscounting, 28, 59, 61, 139–40
social-class differences, 32–4
understanding numerals in the environment, 96–7
using LOGO, 157–8

using magnetic numerals, 139–40; in Tins game, 141–50
see also difficulties, children's and children's representations
programming languages, 152, 153
see also LOGO
'progressive' methods, 8–10, 18, 180
reasons for not implementing, 10
purpose, 168, 170, 177–8
for explaining symbols, 104
for representing addition and subtraction, 75–7, 146–51
for representing quantity, 64
for representing zero, 63–4
for using symbols, 122–30

reaction times, 35
'readiness' to learn, 17
reconstructing mathematics, 152–3
Recorde, R., equals sign, 92, 178
representations, see children's representations and other cultures
Resnick, L. B., 35, 181–2
Rhind papyrus, 91
Roman system of notation, 85–6
Ross, P., 155
Rousseau, J.-J., 171
Russell, B., 171

Saxe, G. B., 82, 83 fig.
Sethe, K., 87 fig.
school mathematics
historical perspective on, 2
implications for, 174–83
lack of practical relevance in, 9
see also formal symbolism and difficulties, children's
school-leavers, 2
Schools Council, 24
Schubauer-Leoni, M. L., 77
Schulz, see Peanuts cartoon
Scottish Primary Mathematics Group, 180
Shuard, H., 9, 46–7
Siegriest, F., 77
Sinclair, A., 77, 96–7, 109, 174
Sinclair, H., 77, 96–7, 109, 174
size of number, 27–32, 61, 122
Skemp, R. R., 40, 41
Slade, M., 158

social-class differences, 32–4
Somerwill, H., 181
Stallard, A., 103–9, 110, 118
Starkey, P., 34–5, 174
strategies in Box task, 27–32
'subitising', 28
subtraction
in Babylonian and Egyptian number systems, 91
and class-inclusion, 15
column subtraction, 113–21
errors in: involving zero, 116–18; 'smaller from larger', 115, 121
pre-school, 24–36
use of concrete materials in, 115–21, 132
written representations of, 72–8, 92–3, 122, 124, 125 fig., 126–8
see also operator signs
'sums', effect of doing, 109–11, 122
symbolic reponse category, 59 fig., 60

tallies, 61, 81, 93
in other cultures, 83–4
produced by children, 58, 61–2
tallysticks, 84
teaching mathematics, see school mathematics
Thorndike, E. L., 17–18
Tins game, 64–72, 141–3
extensions of, 143–50
a week later, 70–2, 141–3
Tizard, B., viii, 33, 48–51
translating, 4, 5, 44, 134, 150–1, 169, 174–5
abstract to concrete, 44–51
affected by 'doing sums', 109–11
concrete to written, 53–78, 128–30, 150
difficulties summarised, 170–1
explicit teaching methods, 178, 180–2
helped by games, 135–8, 150–1
helped by LOGO, 165
helped by magnetic numerals and Tins game, 141–50
hypothetical to written, 124–8
referred to in Cockroft report, 3
related to mathematical ability, 108–9

role of images, 171–4
symbolic to iconic, 124
written to concrete, 98–108, 115–22,
    131–3
see also children's representations
Turtle Graphics, 153
see also LOGO

untaught methods, see non-standard
    methods

VanLehn, K., 115, 117
visualising, 29, 32, 126
Vygotsky, L. S., 93–4, 175

Wallace, J. G., 28
Watson, F. R., 173
Williams, B. J., 90
Williams, G., 2
Williams, M., 181
wolf-bone, Paleolithic, 83

work-book pages, 55 fig.
written arithmetic, 53–78
    nature of the medium, 93
    see also children's representations
        and formal symbolism

Young, A. W., 27–8

Zaslavsky, C., 90
zero
    children's explanations of, 106–7
    children's positioning of in
        sequence, 139
    children's representations of, 62–3,
        65–72, 77–8
    children's use of magnetic '0',
        141–2
    errors involving, 116–18
    and place-value, 89–90
    and puzzlement, 63, 65
    as result of subtracting, 27
    symbols for in other cultures, 89–90